Other books by Ben-Tzion Spitz

Fiction

- Joshua: Conqueror
- Destiny's Call series:
Book One - Genesis
Book Two – Exodus
Book Three - Leviticus
Book Four – Numbers
Book Five – Deuteronomy

Non-Fiction

- Mikraot Ketanot: Torah Shorts on the Weekly Reading
- The Oracle and The Rabbi: A Nexus of Art, Bible and Jewish Philosophy
- Jewish Adventure in Modern China

#rambam #tweets

A compendium of tweet-sized entries from the entirety of Maimonides' Mishne Torah

Ben-Tzion Spitz
@bentzis

Valiant Publishing

Content from TweetYomi.org

A TorahWorks project

#rambam #tweets

A compendium of tweet-sized entries from
the entirety of Maimonides' Mishne Torah

@bentzis

Valiant Publishing, 377 Forest Avenue
Woodmere, NY 11598, USA

Author's websites: tweetyomi.org and torah.works
For schools or bulk orders, contact the author directly at:
bentzispitz@gmail.com
First Edition
1 3 5 7 9 10 8 6 4 2
ISBN 978-1-937623-31-9

To Maimonides, The Great Eagle

Table of Contents

#definitions

#tweets: Messages sent via online news & social media site "Twitter" @twitter.com, (previously) restricted to 140 characters per message.

#RambamYomi: Daily study by worldwide Jewry of one chapter a day from Maimonides' (Rambam's) Mishne Torah. 1,000 chapters. Completed in cycle of around 3 years.

#rambam #tweets: #RambamYomi content squeezed 1 idea / 1 chapter / day into tweet format & presents a compendium from entire Mishne Torah.

#purpose

#RambamYomi is an incredible worldwide phenomenon, educating and uniting Jews off all streams and backgrounds.

#RambamYomi can be a time-consuming, laborious yet intellectually, spiritually, and religiously invigorating commitment.

#RambamYomi can seem intimidating to people with a weak Jewish education.

#RambamYomi is now accessible for people with NO background, translated into English & w/ excellent explanations & commentaries, in print & online.

#methodology

#rambam #tweets are for people who want a brief, tiny, initial exposure to the tip of the Mishne Torah iceberg.

#rambam #tweets is akin to explaining Einstein's Mass-energy equivalence by merely writing $E=mc2$. There is significantly more behind it.

#rambam #tweets just gives a highlight / chapter. It's written in tight shorthand, trying to squeeze a lot of info in < 140 characters.

#rambam #tweets can also be a good and fast review for people who've already learned Rambam's Mishne Torah before.

#technical

#rambam #tweets gives the chapter number and law number before each tweet.

#rambam #tweets should arouse your curiosity. Check out the actual Rambam online in translation to see what it's really talking about.

#rambam #tweets was composed with the help of sefaria.org and chabad.org. Both resources are highly recommended.

#Rambam

INTRODUCTION

#**Intro**

A: Moshe got from God all Laws explicitly; Torah written, rest orally. Transmitted thru generations. List until R' Ashi.

B: Besides leaders, each generation had 1000s also transmitting, until Talmud, dispersion, then different traditions.

C: All must follow Talmud. Geonim wrote responsa. My Mishne Torah only book beside Torah that need. 1108 yrs post-Temple.

#MinyanHamitzvot

A: List of positive commands (Mitzvot Aseh) from number 1 until number 83; of 248 Aseh; of 613 total.

B: List of positive commands (Mitzvot Aseh) from number 83 until number 166; of 248 Aseh; of 613 total.

C: List of positive commands (Mitzvot Aseh) from number 167 until number 248; of 248 Aseh; of 613 total.

D: List of prohibitions (Mitzvot Lo Ta'aseh) from number 1 until number 122; of 365 Lo Ta'aseh; of 613 total.

E: List of prohibitions (Mitzvot Lo Ta'aseh) from number 123 until number 244; of 365 Lo Ta'aseh; of 613 total.

F: List of prohibitions (Mitzvot Lo Ta'aseh) from number 245 until number 365; of 365 Lo Ta'aseh; of 613 total.

#RambamsOrder

A: 1. Mada (Knowledge/Basic), 2. Ahava (Love/Constant), 3. Zmanim (Times/Festivals), 4. Nashim (Women/Marriage).

B: 5. Kedusha (Holiness), 6. Haflaa (Utterances), 7. Zraim (Fields), 8. Avoda (Temple), 9. Korbanot (Sacrifices).

C: 10. Tahara(Purity), 11. Nezikim(Damages), 12. Kinyan(Property), 13. Mishpatim(Judgement), 14. Shoftim(Judges).

1. SEFER MADA

BOOK OF KNOWLEDGE

#**YesodeiHatora**

1:11 God has no body, form; no connection, separation, place or measure. Not in time; no start or end. No change.

2:9 All existence aside from God, from influence of God's truth. God knows everything, nothing hidden from Him.

3:9 Stars & spheres have soul, knowledge, intellect. Alive & recognize God. Know less than angels, more than men.

4:9 Soul isn't of elements. Body dies, decomposes, soul remains. Knows things above matter, God, exists forever.

5:5 Gentiles tell group of Jews: "Give us one of you to kill, or we kill you all," allow selves to be killed.

6:2 7 names of God: YHVH (also ADNY), El, Elo'ah, Elohim, Elohai, Shaddai, Tzvaot. Erase even 1 letter, lashed.

7:1 God conveys prophecy to man. Only on wise sages, strong character/mind, mind overcomes natural inclinations.

8:1 Mt Sinai revelation source of belief in Moses' prophecy. Our eyes saw, our ears heard, Voice of God to Moses.

9:3 Proven prophet (i.e. Elijah) can order temporary violation of commandments, except for permitting idolatry.

10:4 True prophet if future positive predictions always come true. God can revert on negative predictions (Yona).

#**Deot**

1:4 Straight path: midpoint of character traits: not angry, not unfeeling; not stingy, not spender; not elated, not sad.

2:1 Morally ill love bad traits, hate good path, lazy to follow it. Cure: go to wise, soul-healers, teach them good path.

3:3 "Know God in all your ways." Every act, eating, working, sleeping, intimacy, should be to better serve & know God.

4:15 Idle, doesn't exercise, even eats properly, will always have pain. Overeating is like poison & main cause of illness.

5:3 If gets drunk, is a sinner, shameful & will lose his wisdom. If gets drunk in front of others, desecrates God's name.

6:1 Person is influenced by friends, will follow local norms. Should be in company of wise & live in town of righteous.

7:3 3 sins gets punished in this world, no portion in next: idolatry, forbidden relations & murder. Gossip is = to all 3.

#TalmudTora

1:8 Every Jewish man obligated to study Torah: rich, poor, healthy, sick, young or old. Need fixed time day & night.

2:5 Up to 25 students per teacher. 25 to 40 students, teacher + assistant. >40 students, split to 2 teachers.

3:3 There is no other mitzva from out of all the mitzvas that is equal to Torah study. Torah study is equal to all.

4:1 Don't learn from teacher who doesn't follow proper path, even if he's very wise, until returns to proper path.

5:1 Just as honors dad, must also honor Torah teacher, even more. Dad brought into this world, teacher into next.

6:1 Mitzva to respect every Torah sage, even if not one's teacher. Stand for him when within 4 cubits until passes.

7:13 Practice of early generations pious: hear their shame, not answer; pardon, forgive person who insulted them.

#AvodaZara

1:1 Idolatry's start: Enosh's time, people worshiped God's servants, the stars & spheres, built temples, sacrifices.

2:1 Can't serve any creation; even if knows that God is true God, but worships intermediaries, it's still idolatry.

3:3 Always liable if bow, slaughter, sacrifice or libation, no matter what the normal form of serving that idol is.

4:1 City incited to idolatry (Ir Hanidahat): inciters executed by stoning; inhabitants that worshiped, decapitated.

5:3 Don't warn idolatry-inciter; only sinner that we entrap. If incites in front of 2 men, witnesses, inciter stoned.

6:3 Idolatry of Molech: lit fire, gave kid to priest, priest returns kid, dad carries kid between flames. Gets Karet.

7:1 Positive command to destroy idols, accessories & anything made for them. Must eradicate from land of Israel.

8:9 Idol that belongs to a Jew can never be nullified. Forbidden to benefit from it forever. Must be entombed.

9:8 Can't sell item to idolaters if can harm others: bears, lions, weapons, fetters, chains. Can't sharpen weapons.

10:1 If see an idol worshiper being swept away, drowning in river, in any danger, don't help; but don't cause death.

11:16 If believe in validity of occult arts, astrology, etc. foolish, feeble-minded, underdevelopment intellect.

12:7 Beard has 5 corners: upper & lower cheek on both sides & chin. Prohibited to shave w/ razor. Ok w/ scissors.

#Tshuva

1:4 Repentance atones all sins, immediately or over time. Depends how severe. May suffer, need Yom Kipur or death.

2:10 Can't refuse to be appeased. Forgive w/ whole heart. Don't seek revenge or bear grudge. Jew's path, upright spirit.

3:6 No next world: atheists; infidels; deny Torah, resurrection, Messiah; apostate; cause many to sin; leave community.

4:5 Sins that person continues to commit, difficult to abandon: gossip; slander; short temper; evil thoughts & friends.

5:2 All have free will to be righteous/wicked, wise/foolish, merciful/cruel, miserly/ generous or any other traits.

6:5 When God says something will happen in future, man still has free will. Man can't understand how God knows future.

7:3 Also need to repent from bad traits like anger, hate, envy, frivolity, pursuit of money & honor, gluttony, etc.

8:2 World to come: no: body, eating, sitting, sleeping, death, sadness. Eternal joy. Will understand truth of Godliness.

9:1 If fulfill Torah w/ joy, meditate on its wisdom at all times, God will remove all obstacles & grant good to fulfill.

10:3 Ideal love of God: lovesick. Just as lovesick for a woman, obsessed, never stops thinking of her, more for God.

2. SEFER AHAVA

BOOK OF LOVE

#Shma

1:4 Before Jacob died, asked sons if with him in Unity of God, they answered Shma, he answered Baruh Shem. Reason we do.

2:10 Can recite Shma in any language that understand. Must be as careful in enunciation in foreign language as in Hebrew.

3:4 Can't say or even think Shma or any words of Torah or sanctity in bathroom, unclean place or place w/ feces or urine.

4:8 Jews took custom to read Torah, recite Shma even after seminal emission. Just like fire can't be impure, also Torah.

#Tfila

1:2 Biblical command, duty of men & women to pray to God daily. Supplication, praises, request needs, thank for all.

2:1 In R' Gamliel's day, Jewish heretics increased. Greatest need; added Amida blessing asking God to destroy heretics.

3:8 Forgot to pray, unavoidably detained, compensates next immediate prayer time, says Amida 2x. 1st current, makeup 2nd.

4:16 Clear mind of all thoughts, envision standing before God. Don't rush; not burden. Sit a bit before & after prayer.

5:1 Must have or prevents praying: pure hands; cover nakedness; pure place; remove distractions; proper intent of heart.

6:2 Praying w/ public, don't make your Amida too long. Can add in middle blessings related requests: health, income, +.

7:14 Must say 100 blessings/day, upon waking 23, w/ Shma 7, Tzitzit 1, Tfilin 1, Amida 3x18=54, Meals 7x2=14. Total=100.

8:1 Communal prayer always heard, even w/ sinners. God doesn't reject that prayer. Don't pray alone if can w/ community.

9:7 Can't say "Just like God is merciful on law of bird's nest, so should be merciful on us." They're decrees, not mercy.

10:1 Prayed & didn't concentrate, pray 2nd time w/ concentration. Concentrated for 1st blessing, don't need to repeat.

11:1 Wherever 10 Jews live, must set up place to gather & pray at time of each prayer. Can force each other to build.

12:6 Erred while publicly reading the Torah, even in pronunciation of one letter, must repeat until gets it right.

13:25 Obligated to study the Torah portion that community is reading that week; read 2x in Hebrew, 1x in translation.

14:7 Kohens don't look at people when do Priestly Blessing; look down. People should face Kohens, but don't look at face.

15:6 Kohen does Birkat Kohanim even if not careful w/ Mitzvot. Don't tell wicked: be more wicked & abstain from Mitzva.

#Tfilin

1:8 Torah written on Gvil (whole processed skin); Tfilin on Klaf (thin outer layer); Mezuza on Duchsustos (inner layer).

2:1 Head Tfilin: 4 passages on separate parchments in separate compartments. Arm Tfilin: 4 passages on 1 parchment.

3:2 Head Tfilin: wood block mold, width=length, 3 grooves make 4 projections, soak leather, put in mold between grooves.

4:1 Put head Tfilin on skull point, end hairline, spot where can feel baby's brain; knot: top of neck, bottom of skull.

5:8 Can't put Mezuza: on pole; behind door; horizontal in doorpost; deeper than handbreadth; in reed of future doorpost.

6:1 Mezuza home reqs: 4x4 cubits; doorposts; lintel; roof; door; 10Tefah entry; not holy; for humans; dignified; steady.

7:1 Mitzva for man to write Torah scroll for self. Doesn't know how, pay scribe. Wrote 1 letter, as if did whole scroll.

8:4 List Torah's Parsha Ptuha & Stuma (open & closed passages). Used renown scroll of all 24 books in Egypt by BenAsher.

9:10 Torah scroll I wrote: columns 4 thumbbreadths wide, except Sea Song, Haazinu, 6 wide. 51 lines/column, 226 columns.

10:8 Anyone impure, even a menstruating woman or gentile can hold & read a Torah scroll. Torah words can't get "impure".

#Tzitzit

1:8 7-13 segments of Tzitzit, but if wound Tehelet 1x around strands, ok. Ideally, Tehelet around upper 1/3 of strands.

2:2 Tehelet: Hilazon creature, color like sea, put its black blood in pot w/ herbs until bleached wool turns sky-blue.

3:12 Always be careful regarding Mitzva of Tzitzit. Torah considers it equal to all Mitzvot & all are dependent on it.

#Brahot

1:2 Anyone who derives benefit from this world w/o reciting a blessing considered as if misappropriated a sacred item.

2:14 Ate meal, forgot to say Birkat Hamazon after, remembered before food digested, returns & says. Also if not sure.

3:9 Pat Habah Bkisnin: Dough kneaded w/honey, oil, milk or other condiments, baked. Say Mezonot unless establishes meal.

4:1 Say BirkatHamazon where ate. Ate walking or standing, sit down where finished & say. Forgot, remembered, say there.

5:7 Women, servants & kids not included in Zimun for Birkat Hamazon, but can make their own, each group separately.

6:1 Even if hands aren't dirty & not aware that contracted ritual impurity, still shouldn't eat bread until wash hands.

7:5 Bread-breaker gives bread slice to each person. People pick up slice w/ hand. Don't take from hand, unless mourner.

8:2 For fruit juice, say blessing of Shehakol (not Haetz), except for grapes & olives. On wine, grape juice say Hagefen.

9:8 Don't bless over fragrances of: idols; forbidden women; for dead; of toilets or to remove odor; utensils; clothing.

10:26 Pray to God over future, ask for mercy; & thank & praise for all things that have happened. Thank more, better.

11:8 Made Suka, Lulav, Shofar, Tzitzit, Tefilin, Mezuza, don't bless, 'cuz still Mitzva to perform. Bless when perform.

#Mila

1:1 Mila positive Mitzva, punishment Karet: uncircumcised male who doesn't circumcise foreskin, soul cut off from people.

2:1 Mila can be done by slave, woman or minor if no man around. Gentile can't do, but if did, don't repeat. Use knife.

3:2 At end say: Just as you've brought him into the covenant, so, too, may you bring him to Torah, marriage & good deeds.

#PrayerOrder

1: Order of prayer for the entire year.

2: Text of the blessings of Shemona Esre (Amida) and their order.

3: Text of all the intermediate blessings.

4: Text of the confession and text of the grace after meals.

3. SEFER ZMANIM

BOOK OF TIMES

#Shabat

1:1 Prohibition to labor on Shabat. If did on purpose gets Karet; stoned if warned & witnesses; sacrifice if accidental.

2:3 Violate Shabat for dangerously ill. Should be done w/o hesitation by leaders & wise; not non-Jews, women or kids.

3:1 Can start forbidden labor on Friday that continues on own on Shabat & can benefit from what was completed on Shabat.

4:1 Items that add heat when cover food: gefet; manure; salt; lime; sand; damp grape skins, raw wool & grass.

5:3 Shabat candles must be lit before sunset. Women more obligated than men. Unsure if Shabat started, don't light.

6:1 Can't tell non-Jew to perform work on Shabat on behalf of Jew, even if told before Shabat & don't need until after.

7:5 Cut vegetable into small pieces on Shabat, liable; resembles grinding. Grinding: dividing entity into smaller parts.

8:12 Can't separate food from unwanted matter, or 1 food from other on Shabat. Can separate by hand to eat immediately.

9:8 Can't cut nails, hair, mustache or beard on Shabat; derivative of shearing. Can't remove by hand, but not liable.

10:1 On Shabat one can tie a knot that won't stay tied permanently and that doesn't need a craftsman to tie it.

11:15 Wrote on Shabat, only liable if wrote with substance that leaves permanent mark on surface that will preserve it.

12:2 Can't extinguish fire or coals on Shabat. Adds oil to lamp, liable for kindling; removes oil, extinguishing.

13:2 Hand like space 4x4 handbreadths. Took item from person's hand in 1 domain, put in other's hand in 2nd, liable.

14:1 4 domains for Shabat: private; public; Karmelit; Makom Patur. Public: desert, forest, market, road 16 cubits wide.

15:2 Don't stand in private domain extend head & drink from public domain, or in public domain & drink from private.

16:16 Enclosure's open space framed by "entrance", open space not greater than closed space: can carry within enclosure.

17:36 Measurement sizes: Etzba (Fingerbreadth)=thumb width. Tefach (Handbreadth)=4 Etzba. Amah (Cubit)=6 Tefach.

18:16 Liable if transfer live animal from domain. Person not considered a burden if move, but if bound or sick, liable.

19:26 Friday before nightfall, check pockets of clothes in case forgot something there & inadvertently carry on Shabat.

20:3 Jew can't lend or hire his animal to a non-Jew to work with on Shabat. Commanded to have his animals rest.

21:1 "Shvut" ceasing activity on Shabat. Torah gave to Sages to define. Resemble forbidden labors or can lead to it.

22:6 Can pour hot water into cold or cold into hot as long as not on the fire. Can't put spices into boiling pot.

23:4 Can't do action that completes object, "dealing final blow." Can't sound musical tones, with instrument or hands.

24:1 Forbidden to do or even speak on Shabat about weekday & work matters, even if not violating any forbidden labors.

25:3 If can use the utensil on Shabat, can move it. If can't use, can only move for its place, or if have permitted use.

26:16 If fit to be eaten by commonly found animal, can be carried on Shabat. Dry turmos beans for goats, bones for dogs.

27:9 On way to city, if within 2000 cubits of city before Shabat, can walk thru entire city + 2000 cubits on Shabat.

28:19 Servant or maid say Shabat city limit until here, believe. Adult says As child, we went until this place, believe.

29:5 Can't eat, drink wine from Shabat start until Kidush. Can't eat, drink, labor after Shabat until Havdala. Water ok.

30:1 There are 4 dimensions to observing Shabat: 2 Biblical: Remember & Observe. 2 from Prophets: Honor & have Pleasure.

#Eruvin

1:6 Eruv: all join in 1 collection of food before Shabat. Just as share food, share jointly-owned & private property.

2:10 For an Eruv to be established where non-Jews live, a Jew needs to rent the rights to the non-Jew's domain.

3:9 2 Eruvs separated by wall 10 Tefah high. If reduce height of 4 Tefah long part, can set single Eruv for both areas.

4:5 Dad/son, teacher/pupil live in same courtyard, don't need Eruv. They're 1 household, even if don't always eat as 1.

5:22 City belonging to many w/ 1 entry & a ladder in wall, can include entire city in Eruv. Ladder in wall not an entry.

6:24 Bless for Eruv Tchumin like for courtyard Eruv (Hatzerot) & Shituf. Add "can go 2000 Amot in all directions."

7:1 Main establishment of Eruv Tchumin is to go to place by foot on Friday. Sages allowed to establish by sending food.

8:14 If holiday falls on Friday, can't set Eruv Chatzerot or Eruv Tchumin for Shabat on holiday. Rather, do it Thursday.

#**Asor**

1:2 All that can't do on Shabat, can't do Yom Kipur. Difference is punishment if violate Shabat, stoned; Yom Kipur, Karet.

2:9 Yom Kipur: Pregnant woman overcome w/ desire to eat, whisper to her: today is Yom Kipur. Still desires, feed her.

3:1 Can't wash self on Yom Kipur, not with hot or cold water. Not whole body, not one limb; can't even dip pinky in water.

#YomTov

1:4 On Chag, can transfer articles from one domain to another & can kindle fire. Can do labors needed to prepare food.

2:1 Chick hatched on Chag, can't be handled, Muktze. Calf born on Chag, had designated to eat mother, can also eat calf.

3:12 No making cheese on Chag. If make day before, doesn't lose flavor. Can crush spices on Chag, not salt; same reason.

4:20 Can't use scale on Chag, or even use to protect food from mice. Expert butcher not allowed to weigh meat by hand.

5:1 Torah allowed carrying on Chag even if not for food preparation, but can't carry in same way that does on weekday.

6:20 Have joy that involves service of God. Impossible to serve God while in midst of levity, frivolity, or drunkenness.

7:16 Don't marry or do Yibum on Chol Hamoed, so joy of Chag not obscured by joy of marriage. Can betroth w/o a party.

8:17 Work forbidden before Chag, like on Friday afternoons. If works during this time will never see blessing from it.

#HametzUmatza

1:1 If purposely ate olive size of Hametz on Pesah, from night of 15 Nisan until end of 21 Nisan, liable to Karet.

2:19 Has voyage <30 days before Pesah, must search for Hametz before goes; also if >30 & returning before Pesah.

3:11 How does one destroy Hametz? Burn it; crumble & toss to wind; throw into sea. If covered by >3 Tefah of dirt.

4:5 Jew can give Hametz to non-Jew as collateral & say: If I don't bring $ between now & such date, Hametz yours.

5:1 Hametz is only 5 grains: wheat, rye, barley, oats, spelt. Kitniyot: rice, millet, beans, lentils, not Hametz.

6:1 Biblical command to eat Matza night of 15 Nisan. Applies every place & time. Can be eaten whole night.

7:1 Biblical command to relate miracles that occurred to our ancestors on night of 15 Nisan. Even if great sage.

8:7 In Temple would bless (on Zevah) & eat from Hagiga offering (of 14th), then bless & eat from Pesah sacrifice.

#**NusachHahagada:** Entire text of the Maggid portion of the Haggada as is said since destruction of the Temple.

#Shofar+

1:1 Positive biblical command to hear sounding of Shofar on Rosh Hashana. Shofar must be bent ram's horn, nothing else.

2:1 These must hear Shofar's sound: Kohens, Levites, Israelites, converts, freed slaves. Women, slaves, minors, exempt.

3:3 Shofar blast order: bless; Tekiah/Shvarim/Truah/Tekiah x3; Tekiah/Shvarim/Tekiah x3; Tekiah/Truah/Tekiah x3.

4:1 Suka measurements: Height: >10 Tefah, <20 Amot. Area: >7x7 Tefah, no upper limit. Off even by a bit, invalid.

5:1 Suka S'chach: material that grows from ground, detached. Doesn't: become ritually impure, have odor or falls apart.

6:5 Eat, drink, live in Suka 7 days & nights like in home. Consider house temporary and Suka permanent.

7:2 Sukot species: "fruit of beautiful tree" = Etrog. "Boughs of covered trees" = Hadas (myrtle), 3+ leaves/ring.

8:8 Only do Lulav Mitzva w/ own 1st day of Sukot. Give to friend, must be as gift. Can be conditionally. Not w/ kids.

#Shkalim

1:5 Give 1/2 Shekel from 1/2 coin of current currency; at least same value as 160 barley grains of silver. (~$5 today).

2:9 Shkalim set aside to buy sacrifices serve as atonement for entire Jewish people. Includes now & future collection.

3:8 Lost 1/2 Shekel, responsible for it until give to treasurer. City sent w/ messenger & stolen or lost, give again.

4:1 Shekel funds used for: public sacrifices, libations, salt, wood, incense, showbread, red heifer, Azazel goat, +.

#Hodesh

1:2 Difference between 1 solar & lunar year ~11 days. When difference ~30 days, add 1 month to year; called Meuberet.

2:4 Bet Din calculate as astronomers do to know exactly when, where & how new moon will appear. Test truth of witnesses.

3:1 Witnesses saw the new moon: if distance of night & day or less between them & Bet Din, go testify. If further, no.

4:2 Court adds month to year 'cuz of 3 signs: Tkufa; spring; fruits. If Tkufa of Nisan will be on 16Nisan or later, add.

5:3 When did all of Israel start to calculate calendar? End of Talmud sages, Israel destroyed, no permanent Bet Din.

6:2 Day & night are 24 hours. Hour divided into 1,080 Halakim. Divisible by 2, 4, 8, 3, 6, 9, 5, 10.

7:1 Rosh Hodesh Tishrei is never set on Sunday, Wednesday or Friday. If Molad falls on those days, set for next day.

8:2 Lunar months set by days: 29 days, Lacking, several hours shorter than real lunar month; 30 days, Full, more hours.

9:3 Nisan equinox when sun enters Aries. Tamuz solstice, Cancer; Tishrei equinox, Libra; Tevet solstice, Capricorn.

10:1 Sages that say solar year < 365.25 days say its 365 days, 5 hours, 997 units & 48 moments. Moment = 1/76 of unit.

11:7 The heavenly sphere divided into 360 degrees, 12 constellations. Constellation=30 degrees, degree=60 minutes, etc.

12:1 Mean distance sun travels in 1 day: 59 minutes, 8 seconds (59' 8"); in 10 days: 9 degrees, 51 minutes, 21 seconds.

13:1 To know sun's true position on any day, calculate mean position & apogee, subtract apogee from mean = sun's course.

14:1 Moon has 2 mean rates of progress: small orbit not around Earth, within larger orbit around Earth.

15:2 Previous calculations to sight moon. 2x elongation can't be < 5 degrees or > 62 degrees night of moon sighting.

16:1 Part of moon's orbit inclined north of sun's orbit & part south. Intersect at 2 points. At north=head; south=tail.

17:24 Astronomy & geometry calculations from Greeks, now in hands of Sages. Wisdom of Yisachar tribe wasn't transmitted.

18:1 Nights moon won't be sighted 'cuz of clouds; valley; mountain to west. On mountain or on sea, can see even small.

19:4 From Aries, constellations' positions diverge from equator to north until Cancer, 23.5 degrees north of equator.

#Taaniot

1:2 Cry out to God during difficulties, path of repentance, realize 'cuz of bad deeds, repent, difficulties removed.

2:1 Fast, trumpets if: enemies; army; plague; rampage; locust; blight; fallen house; epidemic; no sustenance; no rain.

3:2 If no rain by Rosh Hodesh Kislev court decrees 3 communal fasts Monday, Thursday, Monday. Can eat & drink at night.

4:2 Elders rebuke community on fast, say: it's not sackcloth & fast that have effect, but repentance & good deeds.

5:13 To remember Temple's destruction, women shouldn't have jewelry made w/ all pieces of set; shouldn't be perfect.

#**Megila+**

1:1 Hearing Megilat Esther supersedes learning Torah & all other positive Mitzvot, except burial of Meit Mitzva.

2:1 Read Megila out of order, not good. Read verse 1, skipped 2, read 3, went back & read 2, no good. Read in order.

3:1 Jews suffered greatly under Greek rule. God saved. Hasmoneans overcame them, ruled 200 yrs until end of 2nd Temple.

4:12 Hanuka candle-lighting dear Mitzva. Even if gets food from charity, borrows or sells clothing to buy oil & lamp.

4. SEFER NASHIM

BOOK OF WOMEN

#Ishut

1:3 Once woman Mekudeshet (married) even if not consummated, any man that has relations w/ her liable to court execution.

2:1 Girl from birth-12 years old: Ktana (minor) or Tinoket (baby). 2 hairs grow in pubic area after 12, Naarah (maiden).

3:19 Father shouldn't marry off daughter while minor; wait until matures & she says "I would like to marry so and so."

4:9 If mentally incompetent man marries sane woman, or sane man marries mentally incompetent woman, marriage not binding.

5:2 Man sold item that prohibited to derive benefit from, used $ to consecrate woman, marriage valid, except if idol $.

6:2 4 rules of conditional agreements: 2x stipulation (+ & -); + must be before -; stipulation before deed; achievable.

7:22 Man marries woman, either want to retract, even if do so immediately, retraction of no consequence. They're married.

8:5 Man said I marry u on condition I'm Tzadik, even if complete Rasha, married b'safek; may have had penitent thoughts.

9:4 She had agent accept marriage for her, in parallel she married another man & don't know which was 1st, divorce both.

10:10 Ktuva lost, can't continue living with wife unless writes new document obligating self to requirements of Ktuva.

11:1 Virgin had Erusin: widow, divorce or Halitza, gets 200zuz if remarry. If wed, gets 100zuz. Considered non-virgin.

12:14 Just as must provide wife subsistence, also kids up to 6 years old. Sages decreed provide maintenance until grown.

13:14 Can tell spouse: I don't want your parents or siblings to visit or to live with us; spouse must respect wish.

14:2 Man needs wife's permission to go on lengthy business trips or change professions; they impact his conjugal duties.

15:2 Mitzva of having children is incumbent on man, not wife. If occupied in study of Torah, can delay marriage.

16:1 Nedunya: Property that wife brings to marriage. 2 types: Nichsei Tzon Barzel, man responsible; Nichsei Mlog, she is.

17:17 Woman can sell or gift her Ktuva. If husband dies or divorces her, buyer collects; if she dies 1st, buyer gets 0.

18:1 Widow supported by husband's estate until collects Ktuva. If she remarries, forfeits rights of 1st husband's estate.

19:17 Sons inherit estate but must provide for daughters until grow or marry. Not enough for both, girls have preference.

20:3 Dad dies, leaves son(s) & girl, she gets dowry from estate. Court figures $ would have given. If can't figure, 10%

21:9 Wife breaks utensils during housework, not liable; if was, would be too cautious, wouldn't do tasks, would fight.

22:23 If wife inherited servants, even if old, don't sell, brings honor to her family. Similar w/ olive trees or vines.

23:12 In matters of Ktuva & all similar matters, local accepted custom is a fundamental principle, a basis for judgement.

24:10 Wife committed adultery, violated Torah or Rabbinic law, or had scandalous report, divorce & she doesn't get Ktuva.

25:1 Wife vowed not to eat meat, drink wine, adorn self w/ colored clothing or jewelry, man can divorce & not pay Ktuva.

#Gerushin

1:23 Gett witness doesn't need to know how to read or sign name. More lenient than any other contract. Spares Agunot.

2:20 If law requires man to divorce his wife & he refuses to give Gett, court authorized to beat him until he agrees.

3:5 Man had Gett written but was then secluded w/ wife, can't use Gett; needs new one; but if gave the old one, valid.

4:11 Although a Gett is valid in any language, the universal practice is only to write it in Aramaic with fixed text.

5:2 Divorce is considered a liability for woman. Therefore can't invoke it (serve the Gett) outside of her presence.

6:30 When husband sends Gett to wife, he must still support & provide all stipulations of Ktuva until received.

7:3 Not trusted to deliver Gett: ones mother-in-law; her daughter; 2nd wife; husband's daughter. All others ok.

8:3 Conditional divorce: Write normal Gett w/ no mention of condition. When give, say only effective if condition met.

9:33 Told agent: give wife Gett in such place, did elsewhere, no good. Said will be in such place, did elsewhere, ok.

10:21 Shouldn't marry a woman if plan to divorce her; don't keep her as a wife, or continue to live together with her.

11:25 Just as can't marry woman 3 months after end of 1st marriage, don't marry if pregnant or nursing (24 months).

12:1 Woman says I was married & now I'm divorced, we believe her. The mouth that prohibited her also permits her.

13:10 Jew says I killed so & so, wife can remarry. We accept testimony. Man's testimony not used to incriminate self.

#Yibum

1:7 Maternal brothers only brothers for mourning & as witnesses; not inheritance or Yibum. That's only fraternal bros.

2:9 Eldest bro overseas, younger bro has Yibum obligation. He can't say wait for older bro. He must do Yibum or Halitza.

3:3 Man presumed to have brother, if at time of death says I don't have brothers or he's not my brother, don't believe.

4:6 Halitza: He puts leather shoe w/ heel not sewn w/ linen on right foot, ties strap. Say won't marry; she removes shoe.

5:1 When Yavam gives Yevama a Gett, disqualifies her & brother's other wives from doing Yibum w/ him or other brothers.

6:8 These don't do Yibum or Halitza: SarisHama, androgynous, can't father kids, unique gender; Aylonit, can't have kids.

7:1 2 bros married 2 sisters. Both bros died; don't know which died 1st. Other surviving brother does Halitza w/ widows.

8:1 Married 1 of 2 sisters but unsure which, he dies childless, brother does Halitza w/ both sisters so can marry others.

#Naara

1:2 Seducer: w/ consent. Rapist: against will. In field (can't get help) assume rape. In city (where can), seduction.

2:1 Seducer pays 50 silvers for the pleasure had + embarrassment & damages caused. Rapist pays the above + pain caused.

3:1 Man makes slanderous report about Jewish maiden, found to be false, he's lashed & pays fine of 100 Sela pure silver.

#**Sota**

1:2 Wife secluded w/ man that warned not to, witnesses saw secluded long enough to roast & eat egg, forbidden to husband.

2:1 Wife was warned yet secluded w/ man, not forced to drink bitter water. She can admit adultery. Gets divorce w/o Ktuva.

3:2 Wife who claims innocence told that many have sinned; told biblical examples to make easier for her to admit guilt.

4:19 Man should always be aware of conduct of his wife & kids & warn them, to keep them on good path. If not, sinner.

5. SEFER KEDUSHA

BOOK OF SANCTITY

#Biah

1:1 If has sex w/ one of Arayot, gets punishment of Karet, both man & woman. Besides Karet, some also liable to execution.

2:12 Suspect or rumor that man had sex w/ woman who's Erva to him, shouldn't live on same lane or be seen in same area.

3:3 Kohen's daughter killed by burning for adultery; man strangled. Israelite's daughter married to Kohen, strangled.

4:1 Woman in state of Nida is like other Arayot. Man who has sex with Nida liable for punishment of Karet.

5:3 Uterus where fetus formed, called Source/Room, where Nida or Zava blood emanates. Uterine channel called Antechamber.

6:2 When woman 1st menstruates or during her Veset (normal period), Nida 7 days, whether saw drop of blood or continuous.

7:1 Woman in labor & blood flows, called "blood of throes". If during Nida time, she's Nida. If during Ziva time, pure.

8:2 Before menstruation woman may have a symptom: yawn; sneeze; anxiety by stomach & lower intestines; goosebumps; warm.

9:10 Woman's garment bloodstained: below belt, impure; above belt, pure; on sleeve, if reaches genital area, impure.

10:3 Developed embryo: size of lentil, 2 eyes, size of fly's, apart; 2 nostrils, close to each other; mouth hairsbreadth.

11:16 Ritual impurity, Ervah status doesn't end for woman until immerses in kosher Mikva w/ no separation of skin & water.

12:17 When non-Jew converts & accepts all Torah's Mitzvot, considered Jew in all matters, can marry Jew immediately.

13:5 Nowadays, when non-Jew wants to convert, needs circumcision & immersion. When Temple is rebuilt, brings sacrifice.

14:1 Non-Jew wants to convert. Ask him why. Don't know that Jews persecuted? If says knows & wants anyway, accept him.

15:9 Convert marries Jewess or Jew marries female convert, child Jew in all respects & prohibited to marry Mamzer.

16:12 Male of any species can't take potion to cause loss of sexual potency. Woman permitted to prevent conception.

17:1 3 women prohibited to all Kohens: divorcee; Zonah (defined Ch18); Chalalah (see Ch19). To Kohen Gadol, those 3+widow.

18:7 Adulteress forbidden to husband. Israelite's wife raped, returns to husband. Kohen's wife raped, forbidden to him.

19:17 Says other not Jew, suspect accuser. Person brazen, cruel, hates people, suspect that perhaps not Jew but Givoni.

20:2 Kohen w/ established lineage: 2 witnesses state he's Kohen of unbroken descent of Kohen who served at Temple Altar.

21:2 Man is forbidden to motion w/ hands, feet, eyes, joke, smell perfume or gaze at a woman that's prohibited to him.

22:1 Man forbidden to be secluded w/ any woman that's prohibited to him. Only exceptions are mom w/ son; dad w/ daughter.

#Maachalot

1:2 Chews cud, no teeth on upper jaw. Chews cud, has split hoofs, except camel. Split hoofs, chews cud, except pig.

2:1 Camel, pig, rabbit, hare, chew cud or split hoofs; can't eat them & certainly not any animal w/ no kosher sign.

3:5 Can nurse infant 'til age 4 or 5. If weaned 3+ days & healthy, don't nurse if over 24 months; less, nurses again.

4:8 Can't eat animal (after proper slaughter) if was dead (Nevela) or about to die (Trefa) no matter what the cause.

5:14 Did Shchita, found living fetus in animal, doesn't need Shchita (can kill other way), unless steps on ground.

6:10 Meat doesn't release all its blood unless salted & washed thoroughly. Wash, salt, wash until exit water clean.

7:5 3 types of forbidden fat, liable for Karet if eat: fat on digestive organs; on kidneys; on flanks. Tail-fat ok.

8:11 9 kosher butchers, 1 not, doesn't know from which got, can't eat. Meat found on street & most stores kosher, ok.

9:1 Forbidden to cook meat & milk together, eat it, or benefit from it. Must bury it. Even its ashes are forbidden.

10:2 Hadash (new grain): Can't eat of 5 grains before Nisan 16. Applies in Israel & Diaspora, w/ or w/o Temple.

11:8 If non-Jew touched wine, Jew prohibited to drink it. If was idolatrous non-Jew, can't even benefit from it.

12:17 Jew left non-Jew in store, if Jew comes & goes, wine kosher. If tells non-Jew will travel, wine forbidden.

13:8 Can give wine to non-Jew to safekeep in closed container, if has 2 distinguishing marks, "seal within a seal."

14:13 When eat from forbidden food because of desire or hungry, liable. If lost in desert & nothing else to eat, ok.

15:5 Cases where a forbidden food mixed w/ permitted food is nullified may need ratio of 60:1, 100:1 or 200:1.

16:1 Ratios to nullify forbidden food depends. If leaven, spice or important, slightest amount forbids whole mixture.

17:31 Forbidden to delay relieving oneself; makes soul detestable, besides bringing on self severe illnesses.

#Shechita

1:23 Shochet must check knife tip, sides before slaughter. Pass back & forth on finger & nail. Can't have any blemish.

2:13 Attached knife to water-wheel, correctly cut animal's neck: if man caused water to flow, kosher only 1st turn.

3:1 5 factors disqualify slaughter; Shechita fundamental to guard against: Shehiya; Drisa; Halada; Hagrama; Ikur.

4:2 Jew doesn't know 5 factors that disqualify & laws of Shechita, even if slaughters correctly, forbidden to eat it.

5:2 8 maladies that if affect animal, Trefe & can't eat: Drusa; Nekuva; Haseira; Netula; Psuka; Kerua; Nefula; Shbura.

6:1 Nekuva: if puncture of any size reaches inner cavity of 11 organs, Trefe, can't eat the animal.

7:7 Inflate lungs, if makes sound, place item on it; if flutters, Trefe. Can't find, put in water, if bubbles, Trefe.

8:9 Animal terrified to extent that lung shriveled up: if result of natural phenomena, Kosher; if man-induced, Trefe.

9:1 Psuka: if skin around marrow of spinal cord severed, Trefe. If skin split lengthwise or perforated, Kosher.

10:13 Even if seems animal will live, if has 1 of conditions that Sages listed as making it Trefe, remains forbidden.

11:15 Some rule if lungs have Sirchot, can't eat. Incorrect. Never custom in France, Spain, West; causes great loss.

12:14 Sukot, Pesah, Shavuot, RH: Animal seller must inform buyer if sold mom or daughter so don't slaughter same day.

13:8 Mitzva to send away mother bird applies only to non-domesticated kosher fowl; doves in dovecote, birds in wild.

14:1 Positive Mitzva to cover blood of kosher wild beast or of fowl that slaughtered. Say blessing before covering.

6. Sefer Haflaa

Book of Vows

#Shvuot

1:1 There are 4 types of oaths: futile oaths; false oaths; oaths about a deposit; oaths of testimony.

2:1 Responds Amen to oath or uses any similar language of affirmation to an oath, as if made oath himself & responsible.

3:1 Compelled to take 1 of these 4 types of oaths, exempt. Can take oath if threatened by robber, murderer or taxman.

4:1 Took oath won't eat, ate less than olive-size, exempt. Took oath won't eat this, ate it, even mustard seed, liable.

5:1 Took oath that other will or won't do act, not liable for false oath. Not in his power to keep or nullify. Lashed.

6:3 Can't release self from own oath. Can't release other of oath or vow if wiser person in area. Need teacher's ok.

7:1 Denied claim after plaintiff administered oath, even if didn't say Amen, is like said Amen in this case & is liable.

8:3 Accused of act w/ financial penalty & swears that didn't, liable for oath of deposit, owes principal, but not fine.

9:1 Plaintiff demands witnesses testify to moveable property claim that only they know, they swear don't know, liable.

10:1 If plaintiff's witnesses unacceptable, relative, disqualified or king: denied knowledge, took oath: not liable.

11:2 Forbidden to take oath on any other matter w/ God's name. Whoever does so will be uprooted from this world.

12:1 Took false oath or oath in vain, only receives atonement after gets retribution for desecration of God's name.

#Nedarim

1:16 There are places where people are inarticulate and mispronounce words. When they vow, we follow the local meaning.

2:1 Laws of vows apply whether took vow of own volition or if other stated vow for him & he answered Amen or the like.

3:7 Oath (Shvua) doesn't effect Mitzva; forbids self from entity. Vow (Neder) effects Mitzva; forbids entity on self.

4:3 Seller vowed won't sell for less than 4, buyer vowed won't buy for more than 2, agreed on 3, ok. Just negotiating.

5:3 Ruben tells Simon, Levi's produce forbidden to you; nonsense. Can't forbid what's not his, unless other says Amen.

6:1 Vows off "benefit that leads to food" of friend, can't borrow sifter, strainer, hand mill, oven, any food utensil.

7:2 2 took vow or oath not to benefit from each other, can't use items owned by city: market, bath, synagogue, books.

8:8 Person's intent determines vow. Carrying wool, suffering, vows won't have wool on again; can wear but not carry.

9:1 Follow intent of words used by people in that place, language & time vow or oath taken. Follow local terminology.

10:1 Vowed "won't taste food today," forbidden until nightfall. Vowed "won't taste food for 1 day," forbidden 24 hours.

11:1 Boy @ 12yrs+1day; girl @ 11yrs+1day, took oath or vow, see if know for Whose sake took vow, check that whole year.

12:1 Dad nullifies any vow, oath daughter makes on day he hears it. Husband nullifies if afflicts her, or affects him.

13:23 Vows to improve traits & conduct are good. If glutton vows off meat for a time; drunkard vows off wine; etc.

#Nezirut

1:1 Nazirite vow: lets hair grow, can't cut hair, get corpse impurity or have anything from grapes while Nazir.

2:20 Nazir applies Temple times & after, but must bring sacrifice; so if vows nowadays, needs to be Nazir entire life.

3:13 Samson wasn't complete Nazir; never took vow; forbidden to drink wine, cut hair; but could have contact w/ dead.

4:1 Vowed will be Nazir day Mashiach comes: said on weekday, Nazir immediately; Shabat or YomTov, Nazir right after.

5:13 If Nazir shaves head, liable for 1 set of lashes. If was warned about each hair, "Don't shave," liable for each 1.

6:18 "Tumat Hatehom" impurity of the depths. Human corpse no one knows about, died naturally. If killed, killer knows.

7:1 If Nazir has contact w/ impurity that isn't from actual corpse substance, doesn't invalidate count of prior days.

8:1 Nazir shaving when completes vow in purity: sacrifices male lamb, Olah; ewe, Chatat; ram, Shlamim; 20 Matza loaves.

9:1 Set aside $ for Nazir sacrifices, brought sacrifices, $ left over; use the rest for sacrifices of other Nazirs.

10:1 Can't do 1 shaving to fulfill completion of Nazir vow as well as obligation of emergence from impurity of Tzaraat.

#Arahim

1:3 Arah values: 30days-5yrs, M=5shekel,F=3; 6-20yrs,M=20shekel,F=10; 21-60yrs,M=50shekel,F=30. 61-death,M=15,F=10.

2:3 Pledged worth of hand, see how much worth with hand, without hand, and then gives the difference to Temple treasury.

3:14 Temple treasurers can seize collateral for Arahim or pledges of worth. Take & sell possessions, collect what vowed.

4:27 When field evaluated for Temple treasury to be sold for its worth, announce sale for 60 days, morning & evening.

5:1 Consecrated ancestral field to Temple, Mitzva for owner to redeem it; gets priority. If doesn't want, don't force.

6:2 Can dedicate to Temple: cattle, sheep, Canaanite servants, ancestral fields; don't dedicate everything that owns.

7:1 Can't redeem consecrated items w/ land, servants or promissory notes. Needs to be silver or other movable property.

8:1 Adar 15 court checks needs of community.
Make sure consecrated property collected,
redeemed to maintain God's House.

7. SEFER ZERAIM

BOOK OF SEEDS

#Kilayim

1:5 Grafting mix of trees included in prohibition of mixing species. Also, vegetable to tree or tree to vegetable.

2:16 At 1st, court agents uprooted mixed species. Field owners happy 'cuz cleared. Court made such fields ownerless.

3:15 Cistern, fallow field, fence, path, trench, low-hanging tree, big rock, separate between 2 different species.

4:1 Can plant 2 rows of zucchini next to 2 of squash next to 2 of beans if trench between species, but not 1 row.

5:7 Can't sow vegetables or grain next to vines. Hallowed. Can't benefit from any of it, even straw or vine wood. Burn.

6:1 Sow, maintain vegetables or grain in vineyard, grow 1/200th, all vines & produce in 16 Amah radius become hallowed.

7:5 Row of vines close to neighbor's row, count as vineyard if < 8 cubits apart, even if path passes between them.

8:13 Separating vines, grain/veggies in Israel only. Diaspora: can't sow 2 types of veggies/grain, grape seeds in hand.

9:9 Liable for riding in wagon drawn by different species or for leading them. Even 100 people leading, all liable.

10:12 Can make, sell mixed fabrics; forbidden to wear/cover with them. If not wearing, i.e., a tent, can sit under it.

#Aniyim

1:7 4 gifts left to the poor in vineyard: individual grapes that fell; underdeveloped clusters; Peah; forgotten grapes.

2:20 Field owner left Peah for poor man in front of him, 2nd poor man comes from behind him, takes it; 2nd acquires it.

3:22 All olive trees on 1 side of city are considered as if they're 1 field & 1 portion of Peah should be left for all.

4:12 Doesn't allow poor to collect Leket; allows 1 but not another; gives 1 advantage over 2nd: stealing from the poor.

5:5 Wind blew sheaves to other's field, forgot sheaf there, not Shiheha; it scattered sheaves in own field, forgot, is.

6:9 Many poor, not enough produce to give each one appropriate amount, place all before them & divide among themselves.

7:2 If sees poor person & doesn't give charity, sins. It says: "Don't close your hand against your brother, the poor."

8:3 Took vow to give charity, forgot how much vowed to give, gives until he says "I didn't intend to give this much."

9:10 Charity trustee was owed $ & paid back in market, don't put $ in pocket; put in charity wallet. Can take at home.

10:4 When giving charity, if does so unpleasantly, destroys merit, regardless of amount. Should give pleasantly.

#Trumot

1:6 For land Mitzvot, world divided in 3: Israel; Syria; Diaspora. Israel divided in 2: settled from Babel; from Egypt.

2:3 Seeds that aren't eaten, e.g., radish & onion seeds, exempt from Truma, tithes, because not for human consumption.

3:10 Don't separate Trumat Maaser by estimation. Must be precise in its measure, as it's explicitly stated in the Torah.

4:4 5 don't do Truma; valid if do: Deaf, Mute, Naked, can't hear or say Bracha; Drunk, Blind, can't choose best portion.

5:2 Can use whole onion for Truma even small, can't give 1/2 onion even if large. Can't use 1 kind of produce for 2nd.

6:3 Israelite woman betrothed to Kohen may partake of Truma & other offerings. Sages decreed can only have after Chupa.

7:15 Deaf-mute, Shoteh or minor Kohen, bought servants; they can't partake of Truma. Court or guardian bought them, can.

8:12 Women who can't have Biblical Truma, can't have Rabbinic Truma either. Decree lest they eat of Biblical Truma.

9:5 Kohen frees servant, servant forbidden in Truma w/ transfer of emancipation bill; also, if obligated to be freed.

10:14 Truma fell into 1 of 2 containers, 1 Truma, 1 ordinary produce (Hulin) & don't know which, assume fell into Truma.

11:4 Don't boil Truma wine; it reduces quantity. Don't pickle Truma onions in Truma vinegar; it spoils the vinegar.

12:14 If kneaded dough w/ water that was left uncovered (could be unsafe), it should be burnt even though it's Truma.

13:2 Seah of Truma fell into less than 100 Seah of ordinary produce, entire mixture becomes like Truma. Sell to Kohen.

14:16 2 grain containers, 1 ritually pure, 1 impure, Truma fell in, don't know into which, assume it fell into impure 1.

15:5 When an egg is flavored with spices that are Truma, even its yolk is forbidden, because it absorbs the spices.

#Maaser

1:1 After separating Truma Gdola, separate one tenth of the remaining produce, called Maaser Rishon. Given to Levites.

2:5 Phase of tithing: When the produce will reach stage that it produces seed that could grow, each species at own time.

3:4 Finished work on produce, but didn't bring home, can snack on it b4 tithed. Once it's home, can't eat until tithed.

4:15 Fig tree in courtyard; may eat figs 1 by 1 while exempt from tithing. Gathered figs together; obligated to tithe.

5:14 Cooks, boils or pickles produce; creates obligation to tithe. Smokes produce until can eat; doubt if has to tithe.

6:6 Can't send gifts of Tevel, even one Torah scholar to another. Might rely on the other and cause Tevel to be eaten.

7:2 Says tithes are at barrel bottom, can't drink from top; at top, can't drink from bottom (liquids mix); solids don't.

8:9 Allocated 1 barrel from 100 as tithes, doesn't know which 1; take wine from 100 barrels, mix, give 1 barrel-worth.

9:4 Don't say blessing when separate TerumatMaaser & MaaserSheni from Demai; obligation was instituted out of doubt.

10:5 Man trustworthy, wife not: accept produce, not hospitality. Wife trustworthy, not him: hospitality, not produce.

11:1 Can't sell or send as present Demai to commoner; assists him in partaking of forbidden food. Can to Torah scholar.

12:11 Sells produce in Syria, says it's from Israel, required to tithe it. Says it was tithed, his word is accepted.

13:10 When Sages issued decree of Demai, decree didn't apply to produce from the Diaspora that was brought into Israel.

14:9 Ground loaf of bread into crumbs or ground dried figs & made into a cake, separate tithes for entire quantity.

#Maaser2

1:1 After separate 1st tithe yearly, separate 2nd. Yr 3 & 6 of 7 yr cycle separate tithe for poor instead of 2nd tithe.

2:1 2nd tithe eaten within walls of Jerusalem. Observed whether Temple standing or not, but only partake if standing.

3:11 2nd tithe spoiled to point that inedible (moldy bread, rancid oil), don't have to eat. Its holiness has departed.

4:1 Can redeem produce from the 2nd tithe, according to their worth. Say: "These coins are in place of this produce."

5:6 When redeeming produce from 2nd tithe for more than its worth, additional value not considered as $ from 2nd tithe.

6:9 Found coins in Jerusalem, considered ordinary $; except on pilgrimage festivals, then considered from 2nd tithe.

7:3 Use $ from 2nd tithe only to buy food for humans that grows from the earth or grows from the products of the earth.

8:10 Has ordinary produce in Jerusalem & 2nd tithe $ outside Jerusalem, can switch holiness to the produce & eat there.

9:1 Produce of 4th year (Neta Revai) is holy. Must be eaten in Jerusalem by its owners in the same way as 2nd tithe.

10:1 Neta Revai applies to all plants to which Orlah prohibition applies. If exempt from Orlah then also Neta Revai.

11:1 Positive Mitzva to declare before God after all presents from agricultural products taken. Called Vidui Maaser.

#Bikurim

1:1 24 presents for Kohens. Covenant w/ Aaron for all of them. If Kohen doesn't admit, not part of Kohens or presents.

2:1 Positive Mitzva to bring first fruits to the Temple. Applies only while the Temple is standing, and only in Israel.

3:8 Bikurim in metal container, Kohen takes it, returns container; in reed or grass basket, Bikurim & basket to Kohen.

4:10 Brought Bikurim & they became impure in Temple Courtyard, spill out basket there; doesn't make the declaration.

5:13 Chalah called Truma. Therefore must separate from dough in same location. Can't separate pure from impure dough.

6:9 Gentile & Jew partners in dough; if Jew's portion large enough to be liable for Chalah, it's liable for Chalah.

7:12 Dough from which Chalah hasn't been separated is like ordinary produce, not like Chalah, for ritual purity laws.

8:4 Dough obligated in Chalah when flour, water kneaded, rolled into 1 mass. Spelt like wheat; oat & rye like barley.

9:1 Mitzva if slaughter Kosher domesticated animal to give Kohen foreleg, jaw & maw. Applies at all times & places.

10:8 When sets aside first shearings & they're lost, responsible to make restitution until he gives them to the Kohen.

11:1 It is a positive Mitzva for every Jewish man to redeem his son who is the firstborn of his Jewish mother.

12:15 Can't buy or sell donkey fetus to or from gentile. If did so, exempt from redeeming firstborn & not penalized.

#Shmita

1:1 It's a positive Mitzva to rest from performing agricultural work or work with trees in the Sabbatical year (Shmita).

2:14 Can't build wall between his field & neighbor's field during Shmita. Can build between his field & public domain.

3:1 Law conveyed to Moshe at Sinai that forbidden to work land last 30 days of 6th year, just before Sabbatical year.

4:29 Gentile buys land in Israel, sows it in Shmita, produce permitted to Jew; gentile not commanded to observe Shmita.

5:18 Can't cut off underdeveloped date clusters on Shmita; spoils dates. If won't produce dates, just buds, ok to cut.

6:8 Transfer holiness of Shmita produce only thru sale. If transferred: can transfer again thru sale or oral assignment.

7:18 Poor permitted to enter orchards up until the 8th year, until the 2nd rains, to gather Shmita fruits.

8:20 Permitted to borrow Shmita produce from the poor. They should be repaid with produce in the 8th year.

9:1 Positive Mitzva to nullify debts on Shmita. If demands payment of debt after Shmita passed, violates prohibition.

10:16 The Jubilee year (Yovel) releases land at its beginning, while Shmita does not release debts until its conclusion.

11:2 Sold field for 60 years, not returned on Yovel. Only returned on Yovel if sold w/o qualification or in perpetuity.

12:1 Sold house in walled city, may redeem it for 12 months from day sold. All $ returned, doesn't deduct anything.

13:6 Don't destroy home to make it into a garden, nor should plant a garden in his ruin, lest one destroy Israel.

8. SEFER AVODAH

BOOK OF SERVICE

#BetHabehira

1:1 Positive Mitzva to build House for God, prepared for sacrifices to be offered within. Celebrate there 3x/year.

2:2 Universally accepted that where David & Solomon built Altar is where Abraham built altar to sacrifice Isaac.

3:5 The Menora should never be made of fragments of broken vessels, whether it was made of gold or of other metals.

4:13 Temple's upper story had 2 beams to climb to roof. Posts differentiated between Kodesh & KodeshKedoshim roof.

5:2 5 gates led to Temple Mount: west 1; east 1; north 1; south 2. Each gate 10 Amot wide, 20 Amot high, w/ doors.

6:16 Temple & Jerusalem sanctified for eternity, comes from Shechina. Rest of Israel sanctified by Jewish conquest.

7:1 Mitzva to hold the Temple in awe. It isn't the physical building which must be held in awe, but rather, God.

8:1 Positive Mitzva to guard Temple. Applies even if no fear of enemies or thieves; expression of respect.

#KleiHamikdash

1:1 Positive Mitzva to prepare anointing oil so that it'll be ready to use for articles that require anointing.

2:12 When Ark transported, shouldn't be on animal or wagon. Mitzva for it to be carried on one's shoulders.

3:11 When Levi performs Kohen's service or assists in task that's not his, liable to death at the hand of heaven.

4:2 Must show Kohens honor, priority for all holy matters: read Torah, say blessings & get desirable portion 1st.

5:1 Kohen Gadol should surpass his priestly brethren in beauty, power, wealth, wisdom, and appearance.

6:10 Gave wood for Altar, can't have eulogies, fast or do Melacha that day (like w/ sacrifice: private festival).

7:7 The appointed over the cymbal would arrange all the musicians who would help Levites w/ their instruments.

8:1 3 types of priestly garments: ordinary Kohen's garments & Kohen Gadol's golden garments & white garments.

9:2 Letters of Tzitz projected outward. Craftsmen engraved letters on plate back while it was pressed to beeswax.

10:5 Kohen lacking garments is liable to die & invalidates service he performs; so too, if wears extra garments.

#BiatHamikdash

1:9 Kohen let hair grow long, doesn't disqualify service. Even though obligated to die, their service is valid.

2:1 Kohen Gadol enters Kodesh Kodashim each year only on Yom Kipur. Kohen enters Sanctuary for service every day.

3:4 Impure because of contact with human corpse, & even a corpse itself, permitted to enter the Temple Mount.

4:10 Communal sacrifices have a fixed time when must be offered; supersedes Shabat observance & corpse impurity.

5:11 Immersed hands, feet in Mikveh or spring, not considered sanctification. One must wash them from a utensil.

6:3 Physical blemishes from birth or acquired, whether will heal or won't, disqualify Kohen's service until heal.

7:13 Kohen w/ bad body odor or breath, desecrates his service like one who has any other physical bodily blemish.

8:16 One who's deaf, intellectually or emotionally unstable, epileptic, depressed, disqualified from priesthood.

9:2 Non-Kohen liable to death in Temple if: sprinkles; lights altar; pours water on Sukot; pours wine on altar.

#IsureMizbeah

1:4 Consecrates, slaughters, pours blood or burns blemished animal for offering, liable for lashes.

2:5 Unfit for sacrifice: 5 or 3 legged animal; hoof like donkey; unsplit hoof; hoof & fibers shriveled up.

3:6 Animal set aside for pagan purposes, or was worshiped, not permitted as offering. If kosher, can be eaten.

4:3 Animal trained to gore until it killed a person, ok as an offering. Considered compelled against its will.

5:11 Must salt offering meat thoroughly, like salting meat before roasting, but even 1 grain is acceptable.

6:15 Meal+wine offerings can be from produce out of Israel; previous year's grain ok; except for Omer, 2 loaves.

7:1 Even if technically not unacceptable for sacrifices (i.e. low quality) must give God highest possible quality.

#MaaseHakorbanot

1:15 Communal offerings: male animals. Chataot: goats/cattle, never sheep. Olot: sheep/cattle, never goats.

2:2 Only animal Olot (burnt-offering) or Shlamim (peace-offering) need accompanying offerings of wine & flour.

3:13 Semicha must be done with all his power, placing both hands on animal's head, not on neck or side of face.

4:6 General rule: Mitzva intended for daytime can do all day; for night can do all night. Should still hasten.

5:2 Slaughter & sprinkle blood of sacred offerings north of altar; less sacred offerings throughout Courtyard.

6:2 Wool, hair, bones, sinews, horns, hoofs offered on altar if connected to animal. Separated, don't offer.

7:7 Must squeeze out blood of bird Chatat. Only blood goes on altar, rest eaten by Kohens like animal offering.

8:19 If Chatat blood gets on garment & taken out of Courtyard, should be returned to Courtyard & washed there.

9:15 If 2 people bring a peace-offering in partnership, one should perform Tenufah with the other's permission.

10:18 Kohen Gadol may partake of any sacrifice w/o division having been made; he may take whatever he desires.

11:2 Liable if ate olive-sized portion of Olah, which can include combination of fat, meat, flour, oil, wine.

12:21 Baked meal-offerings, mix w/ lukewarm water, watched so don't leaven. Kohens are fast, prevent leavening.

13:2-4 Isaron loaves: divide in 12, bake & fry lightly. Divide loaf in 2, for AM & PM offering w/ frankincense.

14:3 If he set aside a Mincha for merit of his 2 sons but he died before bringing it, they may both bring it.

15:2 If designated an animal's heart as Olah, then whole animal is an Olah, since life dependent on that organ.

16:2 Vowed to bring black colored animal, brought white; vowed white, brought black; didn't fulfill obligation.

17:2 Vowed Mincha of flat frying-pan but brings 1 baked in deep pan, accepted, but didn't fulfill obligation.

18:5 Slaughters sacrificial animal outside Temple & offers it there, liable 2x: for slaughtering & offering.

19:1 Offers sacrifice outside Temple on stone or rock, exempt. "Sacrifice" applies on altar, intended for God.

#TemidinUmusafim

1:1 Commandment to offer two lambs as offerings daily. Called Temidin. 1 in the morning & 1 in the afternoon.

2:15 To remove ashes from Temple Mount not "service," but Kohen with disqualifying blemishes shouldn't do.

3:2 If altar was removed, incense should still be offered at spot. If incense flies off altar, don't return it.

4:4 Kohens count by fingers they stuck out, not by people. Forbidden to count Jews except via something else.

5:1 Positive commandment to arrange the showbread (Lechem Hapanim) on the golden table before God in Sanctuary.

6:10 If RoshHodesh falls on Shabat, RoshHodesh song has priority over Shabat one, to publicize that RoshHodesh.

7:23 Forgot, didn't count Omer at night, count during day. Count when standing; but if did sitting, fulfilled.

8:7 Shavuot's 2 loaves dough made & shaped outside Temple, but baked inside Courtyard like all meal-offerings.

9:12 Sacrifices that get precedence regarding being offered also receive precedence with regard to being eaten.

10:6 Each day of Sukot, water libation poured on altar, as separate libation together w/ morning wine libation.

#PsuleiHamukdashim

1:3 If slaughtering sacrificial animals, w/o intent to slaughter, but merely busying himself, disqualified.

2:7 Kohen sprinkling sacrifice blood on altar, hand cut off b4 blood reached space above altar, not accepted.

3:4 If took animal up to top of altar alive, should bring down. Not yet fit to be consumed by altar's pyre.

4:6 Set aside pregnant animal as Chatat, gave birth, it & offspring considered as 2 animals set aside for it.

5:5 Set aside 2 $ piles as surety to purchase Chatat, get atonement with 1, 2nd use for freewill offerings.

6:2 Sacrificial animals got mixed up w/ forbidden ones. Go to pasture until blemished, sell, use $ for new.

7:10 When a bird Chatat is brought because of doubt, it should be offered as required; not eaten, but burnt.

8:8 2 people buy 2 doves jointly or give $ for them to Kohen, he offers whichever wants as Chatat & as Olah.

9:1 Dove from unspecified group flies away, or to doves to be offered, or dies, 2nd dove taken for its pair.

10:5 Sin-offerings (Chatat) that are offered because of a doubt, should not be eaten, but are burnt.

11:3 If while taking handful of meal-offering lifted up pebble, salt grain, or frankincense, disqualified.

12:7 Offered sacrifice for purpose other than for which it was consecrated, accompanying offerings go w/ it.

13:1 3 improper intents disqualify sacrifices: for different purpose, improper place or improper time.

14:5 Sacrificial parts that can't be eaten, but go on Altar's pyre: blood, Eimorim, Olah meat, Minha handful.

15:5 Intent for sacrificial purposes can disqualify sacrificial animals, but for ordinary purposes doesn't.

16:1 Disqualifying intent regarding place, sacrifice disqualified, but not Pigul; regarding time, is Pigul.

17:7 Disqualifying intent for Toda-offering causes bread that accompanies it to be Pigul, not vice versa.

18:18 If impure person partakes of the fats and organs to be offered on the Altar, he is liable for Karet.

19:2 Sacrifice Pigul or disqualified, burnt in Temple immediately. If doubt, left until next day, then burnt.

#YomKipur

1:1 Yom Kippur: total of 15 animals brought as sacrifices including special ones of Kohen Gadol & 2 daily Tamids.

2:7 Kohens & people heard God's explicit name from Kohen Gadol, prostrated, said: Baruh Shem Kvod Malhuto Leolam Vaed.

3:1 2 lots: 1 said "for God" 2nd "for Azazel," same size & material; in container that Kohen Gadol can put 2 hands in.

4:1 Lottery of 2 goats: ties red cord on head of goat to Azazel, faces it toward dessert; ties cord on other's neck.

5:15 Goat died pre-lottery, take new 1 as pair for remaining 1. Died post-lottery, need 2 new goats, do-over lottery.

#Meila

1:11 If slaughters firstborn or consecrated animal, may pull off wool from either side of neck to make space for knife.

2:15 Can't benefit from ashes of the inner altar or ashes of the Menorah, but prohibition of Meila doesn't apply to them.

3:12 Can't benefit from milk or eggs of animals/fowl consecrated as sacrifices for altar; but if did, it's not Meila.

4:7 Used money for Chatat before offered it: add 1/5 to amount benefited, bring Chatat with the money & offer Asham also.

5:8 When consecrating forest, Meila applies to its entirety; the trees, nests at the tops of the trees, or between them.

6:11 Spent consecrated $ for own needs thinking it was ordinary $, violated Meila even if not spent for ordinary matters.

7:9 If consecrated money was entrusted to a homeowner, who then spends it, he violates the prohibition against Meila.

8:3 Consecrated property shouldn't be given as payment for work; can if it's holiness is first "transferred" to money.

9. SEFER HAKORBANOT

BOOK OF SACRIFICES

#KorbanPesah

1:1 Positive Mitzva to offer KorbanPesah on 14th of Nisan, only from 1 yr old lambs/goats. Men and women obligated.

2:2 Can sacrifice KorbanPesah for self alone, if capable of eating it in its entirety; better not to do for just 1.

3:2 Sent an agent to slaughter KorbanPesah, either kid or lamb; agent forgot which, should slaughter both kid+lamb.

4:5 Set aside KorbanPesah, he dies, son can't bring it as a KorbanPesah, but as Shlamim, unless was counted w/ him.

5:7 Non-Jew who converted or kid who comes of age between 1st & 2nd Pesach: obligated to offer 2nd Korban Pesach.

6:1 If couldn't have KorbanPesah on 15 Nisan because was impure, prevented from offering until 2nd Pesah (15 Iyar).

7:2 If 1/2 Israel ritually pure, 1/2 impure, all offer KorbanPesah, but separately. If >1/2 impure, all together.

8:5 If partook of an olive-sized portion of KorbanPesah while it is still day, he violated a positive Mitzva.

9:8 Uncircumcised person who ate an olive-sized portion of Korban Pesach is liable, but can eat Matza & Maror.

10:1 If breaks a bone in a pure Korban Pesach, liable for lashes; if brought in a state of impurity, not liable.

#Hagiga

1:10 Set aside burnt-offering brought when appearing before God for the festival & he died, heirs obligated to offer it.

2:12 Slaughtered celebratory peace-offerings (Shalmei Simha) before festival & ate during festival, fulfills obligation.

3:7 If Hakhel falls on Shabat, gathering delayed 'til after; trumpets, supplications don't override Shabat restrictions.

#Bechorot

1:1 Positive Mitzva to set aside all males first born of the womb, whether among humans, kosher animals or donkeys.

2:1 If any blemishes that disqualify consecrated animals is contracted by 1stborn animal, may slaughter in any place.

3:1 Slaughtering firstborn animals that have blemishes can only be authorized by expert appointed by the Nasi.

4:2 Bought fetus of gentile's cow, or sold fetus of his cow to gentile, forbidden, but exempt from 1stborn status.

5:3 If firstborn of doubtful status, allowed to pasture until it becomes blemished & then may be eaten by its owner.

6:3 All are obligated in the tithing of their animals: Kohens, Levites, and Israelites.

7:5 Don't tithe animals born 1 yr w/ animals born 2nd yr just as don't tithe crops from new yr for crops from past yr.

8:15 Tithed animal jumped back into corral, mixed with others, all left to pasture until get blemish, then eaten.

#Shgagot

1:1 Inadvertently violated negative commandment for which liable for Karet, obligated to bring a sin-offering (Chatat).

2:11 Slaughtered Korban Pesach on Shabat for sake of another sacrifice in error, exempt, the sacrifice is acceptable.

3:10 Yom Kippur, Chatat & guilt-offerings don't generate atonement unless repents & believes in atonement they grant.

4:1 If performed many transgressions for which required to bring a sin-offering, liable for every individual sin.

5:1 If intimate with woman who is forbidden to him many times in one lapse of awareness, liable only for one Chatat.

6:3 Got two cups of animal blood and drank them both in one lapse of awareness, he is liable for only one sin-offering.

7:4 If forgot that the day is Shabat & also forgot that labors were forbidden, only liable for one sin-offering.

8:1 Sin that liable for a fixed Chatat but transgressed inadvertently, liable for Asham Talui if unsure if violated it.

9:3 If 9 yr-old is intimate w/ consecrated maidservant, she's liable for lashes & he's obligated to bring a sacrifice.

10:3 When person afflicted by Tzaraat becomes purified, he must bring 3 animals as sacrifices: two sheep and a ewe.

11:4 Unresolved question: if an impure person suspended self in the space above Temple Courtyard, if part of Courtyard.

12:1 High Court ruled wrong, nation sinned: Court brings Chatat, even if didn't sin; nation doesn't, relied on Court.

13:2 Members of Sanhedrin who act according to the ruling aren't counted in determining if majority followed ruling.

14:3 Court ruled Shabat ended because confused by cloud cover, then sun appeared, not mistaken ruling, but an error.

15:10 Ate half Kzayit forbidden fat while ordinary person & half after became Nasi in one lapse of awareness, exempt.

#MechusareiKapara

1:13 Woman brought Chatat after giving birth, then died, her heirs bring it even if she didn't separate it.

2:8 If Zav had interruption of entire day between 1 discharge & 2nd, not linked together, not considered Zav.

3:2 If Zav has emission during 7 clean days that he's counting, only nullifies that 1 day of his count.

4:2 Got Tzaraat, delayed & didn't shave on 7th day, must wait to immerse & bring sacrifices until he does.

5:7 Did 7 sprinklings w/o proper intent, doesn't find favor Above, but afflicted person regains purity status.

#Temurah

1:7 When either a man or a woman seeks to transfer the holiness of a sacrificial animal, the transfer is effective.

2:1 Transferring holiness of sacrificial to ordinary animal, owner needs to specify from which animal to which animal.

3:1 Animal to which holiness of an Asham was transferred, left to pasture until it contracts a disqualifying blemish.

4:2 The offspring of a sin-offering, & needless to say the offspring of its Temurah, should be consigned to death.

10. SEFER TAHARAH

BOOK OF PURITY

#TumatMet

1:1 Human corpse imparts ritual impurity that persists minimum 7 days when touched, carried or under same structure.

2:12 Corpse's blood imparts impurity like corpse itself when touched, carried, or one is under the same structure.

3:10 When corpse's flesh becomes powdery & flourlike, it's ritually pure. Also, ashes of corpse that was burnt.

4:6 If a Kzayit of fat that was intact was liquefied, it's impure. If it was separated & it was liquefied, it is pure.

5:1 All entities - human or utensils - that become impure from contact w/ human corpse get impurity that lasts 7 days.

6:2 Utensils made of animal turds, stone, or earth, don't get ritual impurity, not by Scriptural or Rabbinical law.

7:5 If corpse impurity flush with covering, impurity pierces through & ascends to heavens and descends to depths.

8:3 Can sow any type of seed in field of lost grave - roots don't reach grave. Don't plant trees, roots do reach.

9:4 Impurity laws don't apply to gentile graves. If touch their grave, still pure, unless touched or carried corpse.

10:1 BetHapras: place where grave was plowed over. Corpse's bones crushed & dispersed throughout field; field impure.

11:6 Syrian ground impure like the Diaspora. Its open space is pure, because a decree was not imposed concerning it.

12:2 Impurity on top of a wooden board: all implements under are pure; the Ohel (barrier) intervenes between impurity.

13:6 Tied a ship to item to anchor it or covered the corner of a garment with a stone, conveys ritual impurity.

14:1 Impurity doesn't enter or depart a shelter if there is an opening less than a handbreadth by a handbreadth.

15:2 Blocked window w/ entity not susceptible to ritual impurity, doesn't intend to move it, window considered closed.

16:1 If there's an opening in house roof & there's impurity under the roof, space directly below the opening is pure.

17:2 Projection surrounds entire building & encompasses handbreadth at entrance to house, it conveys ritual impurity.

18:2 When person looks out from a window & leans over impurity, he makes the entire house where he's located impure.

19:1-6 A beehive-like container interacts with impurity in many different ways due to the hollow spaces inside of it.

20:2 If object swallowed, pure items don't become impure. If dog ate human corpse flesh, entered house, house is pure.

21:2 Upside-down funnel protects anything it covers from impurity. Though its other end has a hole, considered closed.

22:3 Earthenware container protects contents from impurity if sealed close unless has hole big enough for pomegranate.

23:2 Person was placed inside cask that was sealed close, he's pure. Even if the cask was made a covering for a grave.

24:4 Impurity in wall between 2 houses, house closest to impurity is impure. If impurity equidistant, both impure.

25:10 Woman discharged placenta, house in which she's in is impure. Presume there's no placenta without a fetus.

#ParahAduma

1:1 Mitzva of red heifer to offer it year 3 or 4 of life. If older, ok, but don't wait, lest its hairs turn black.

2:2 7 days before burning of red heifer, Kohen who'll burn it isolated from home, like KohenGadol before YomKipur.

3:1 Red heifer only burnt outside Temple Mount, on Mount of Olives. Ramp built from Temple Mount to Mount of Olives.

4:4 If received red heifer's blood in a container, unacceptable. Mitzvah performed with finger, not with a utensil.

5:1 All involved in offering red heifer from beginning to end become impure and impart impurity to their garments.

6:1 The water needed for red heifer's ashes must be drawn only with a vessel, & only from a spring or flowing river.

7:1 When drawing water for red heifer ritual, must focus; any other activity done at same time disqualifies water.

8:1 Carrying water for red heifer ashes, stops to give directions or kill non-threatening snake, water disqualified.

9:5 Sponge in water when placed ashes on it, water in the sponge is disqualified because it's not in a container.

10:7 Must have intent to sprinkle the water on impure person to purify him. If sprinkled without intent, invalid.

11:3 It is acceptable for all of those who are impure to have this water sprinkled upon them.

12:5 If 2 articles are joined together & considered 1 entity, considered as joined for both impurity and sprinkling.

13:4 When only hands became impure, entire body considered to have contracted impurity & must immerse in a Mikveh.

14:3 If earthenware container w/ red heifer ashes placed anywhere impure, ashes become impure regardless of seal.

15:1 Any person or article which touches sanctified water other than for sprinkling to purify, contracts impurity.

#TumatTzaraat

1:1 When there's a Tzaraat affliction of human skin, skin turns as white as the membrane of an egg or whiter.

2:3 Impure for any shade of white in hair (on white skin), whether white as snow or very weak shade of whiteness.

3:2 Healthy flesh imparts impurity regardless of shade; can be red, black, or white if not 1 of 4 shades of white.

4:1 The increase of a blemish imparts impurity regardless of size, as long as was of shades that impart impurity.

5:2 Suffered burn from hot springs of Tiberias, olive dregs, or the like, the affliction is considered as a boil.

6:1 The red portions of the lips are considered as "hidden places" and cannot incur impurity from blemishes.

7:5 Healthy flesh began to be revealed & grow, & Tzaraat shrinks, still impure until Baheret is smaller than Gris.

8:5 2 short golden hairs sign of impurity, whether next to or distant to each other, if can pull out by tweezers.

9:1 All can be impure of Tzaraat blemishes, even a newborn baby or servants, but not gentiles or resident aliens.

10:2 Removed impurity signs/burns healthy flesh before Kohen inspection, pure; after deemed impure, still impure.

11:1 The purification of a person afflicted with Tzaraat is a positive Mitzva and so is his shaving.

12:10 Colored garments don't get impurity due to Tzaraat blemishes, whether naturally or artificially colored.

13:7 Inspecting creased sheet for Tzaraat, its creases are straightened out and then its blemishes are inspected.

14:5 Don't open windows in closed house to inspect its blemishes. If not visible in its present state, it is pure.

15:4 Blemish on wall between 2 houses, both must remove the stones; scrape away mortar, and bring other stones.

16:4 If holds hand over a blemished stone or a blemished stone is held over him, he is pure unless he touches it.

#MetameiMishkavUmoshav

1:4 A male minor can contract Zav impurity at the age of one day.

2:4 Zav bites into zucchini, cucumber, 1 who moves it is impure, b/c liquid from Zav's mouth mixes w/ it.

3:9 Fetus sticks out his hand from womb, his mother contracts the impurity of a woman who gave birth.

4:11 Bloodstained garment treated with 7 detergents, then immersed in the Mikva and deemed pure.

5:1 Zav, Zava, Nida, woman post-birth impure; pass it to humans, items that sit or lie on, until immerse.

6:2 Impure item of Zav becomes prime source of impurity. Imparts impurity to person or Kelim if touched.

7:1 Zav imparts impurity 5 ways: standing, sitting or lying above item, hanging from, or leaning on it.

8:3 If a Zav touches a firmly sealed earthenware container, it remains pure. If moves it, becomes impure.

9:1 Whatever falls as a direct result of the power of the Zav's movement becomes impure.

10:1 An unlearned Jew is assumed to be impure. His clothes are considered a Midras if touched pure items.

11:2 If unlearned Jew brings Kohen barrel of Truma wine or oil, shouldn't accept it, assume it's impure.

12:4 If put Kelim in bathhouse locker & locked it, Kelim are pure, even if gave key to an unlearned Jew.

13:3 Impurity in front of olive-press workers, grape harvesters, if they say didn't touch it, believed.

#SharAvotHatuma

1:1 Animal carcass: primary source of impurity. Touched animal carcass: person primary derivative of impurity.

2:2 Put hand into animal womb, touched dead fetus, considered pure until removes the stillborn animal from womb.

3:5 Wrapped Kzayit portion of fowl carcass of kosher species in lettuce or the like & swallowed it, he's impure.

4:3 No minimum size for Sheretz limbs to impart impurity. To impart impurity a limb of a Sheretz must be intact.

5:2 The semen of a minor does not impart ritual impurity until he is nine years old.

6:7 Offering brought to a false deity imparts impurity when touched & when carried; like carcass of dead animal.

7:3 Sages decreed that impure liquids impart impurity to containers via inner surfaces of the container.

8:1 Rabbinic decree: touched primary derivative of impurity with hands, only hands, until his joints are impure.

9:8 Although forbidden to do so, if wrote Hallel or Shema for a child to study, it imparts impurity to hands.

10:9 Rabbinic law: foods may become third degree derivatives or fourth degree derivatives of impurity.

11:6 If foods joined together by liquid, are joined with regard to contracting impurity associated with foods.

12:7 All food in container considered as joined with regard to consecrated food, but not with regard to Terumah.

13:4 Found utensils in market, street, even desert, assume impure, may have impurity from corpse or Zav.

14:7 If had doubt if liquids imparted impurity to other entities, they're considered pure. Liquid itself impure.

15:11 2 witnesses tell person: You contracted impurity. He says: I'm pure. His word accepted about own status.

16:8 Kid next to cemetery holding roses, even if roses only from impure place, he's pure because there's doubt.

17:5 Creeping animal carcass on piece of dough that broke off of larger quantity, that piece alone is impure.

18:9 When a person loses an article and finds it at home, it is pure, because it can be assumed to be protected.

19:3 Impure loaf mixed w/9 pure. 2 groups of 5 ate loaf each. Group 1 impure, can't pin on others. Group 2 pure.

20:1 Any place designated as a public domain for Shabat is also considered a public domain for laws of impurity.

#TumatOchlin

1:2 These are the 7 liquids that make foods susceptible to impurity: water, dew, oil, wine, milk, blood, and honey.

2:23 If snow became impure & portion joined Mikvah waters, since portion became pure, becomes pure in its entirety.

3:8 If Kzayit of human corpse covered w/ dough, entire amount imparts severe impurity associated w/ human corpse.

4:8 A puffy bread is measured as it is. If it has a cavity, the cavity should be compressed.

5:18 Collected carob seeds w/intent of eating them: aren't susceptible to impurity. Cooked w/intent of eating: are.

6:1 When shells of nuts, almonds are cracked, they're considered attached to the food until the shell is shattered.

7:1 A column of liquid being poured is not considered as joined, neither to an impure entity nor to a pure one.

8:11 Cooked a vegetable w/ Truma oil, person who immersed that day touched it, disqualifies only place he touches.

9:6 Wood absorbed impure liquids, used as fuel for oven, oven is pure; liquids insignificant if absorbed in wood.

10:3 Blood of crawling animal is like its flesh: imparts impurity, but doesn't make foods susceptible to impurity.

11:9 Storing olives in 2 olive presses, completed loading 1 press, they become susceptible to ritual impurity.

12:10 When fruits fell into water & one extended his hand and took them, they don't become susceptible to impurity.

13:2 Person/animal feet get muddy, cross river, rinse them: If happy, water on feet considered uprooted willfully.

14:13 Shook vegetables w/ liquid on them & it descended from upper ones to lower ones, not susceptible to impurity.

15:6 Streams of rainwater that are still flowing, even if don't contain 40 Se'ah, don't contract ritual impurity.

16:6 Produce is considered pure, even from gentile, unless produce type that assumed got susceptible to impurity.

#Keilim

1:3 Utensils from bones or hide of sea-animals, pure. Everything from sea, pure, not susceptible to any impurity types.

2:8 Bundled a pearl in a hide, removed it & a hollow is left, it is susceptible to impurity until it is smoothed out.

3:3 Glass chests, counters, closets: pure. Other glass containers susceptible to impurity. Stringency of glass vs wood.

4:6 Metal ring with coral signet, susceptible to impurity. Coral ring with metal signet, not susceptible to impurity.

5:3 Lyre is susceptible to impurity. Levites' Temple lyres: pure. Guitar, standing harp & drum, susceptible to impurity.

6:1 Impure Kli broken beyond use regains purity by being broken. Pure broken Kli's pieces not susceptible to impurity.

7:13 When a shoe was damaged, if it does not cover the majority of the foot, it is pure.

8:14 Wherever bells are found, they're susceptible to impurity, except in large cities; majority there made for doors.

9:12 When a chain has a lock, it is susceptible to impurity. If it is meant to secure an entity, it is pure.

10:3 Bloodletter's needle, the utensil with which he draws blood, is susceptible to impurity. A sundial pointer is pure.

11:13 Broken or scratched metal mirror: if doesn't reflect majority of face, it's pure. Reflects majority: still a Kli.

12:14 Hole made in upper portion of a large pot or a bowl, it is impure. If it is in its lower portion, it is pure.

13:9 Neither oven, range, or other cooking places contract impurity unless impurity is found from the sealing & inward.

14:4 Rooster swallows dead crawling animal or human corpse flesh, then falls inside an oven: oven is pure, until dies.

15:10 Furnace to make lime, glass, or pottery, pure. Oven w/ side opening & border on its side, susceptible to impurity.

16:10 When the crack in an oven is positioned in a corner, even though one smeared clay at the sides, it is pure.

17:1 Kli accessories are considered as the Kli itself. If Kli contracts impurity, its needed accessory is also impure.

18:3 Homeowner's funnel pure. Perfumer's funnel can be impure: its turned on its side for customers to smell fragrance.

19:15 Kettle w/ hole patched w/ tar, pure, can't hold hot liquids as it holds cold ones. Kli made of tar, beeswax, pure.

20:2 Coated earthenware container for cooking, coating isn't joined to it. Coated to heat tar, is as if joined to it.

21:4 Plumb lines used by roofers and artists are impure regardless of their length.

22:15 If head covering is torn, if it no longer can cover greater portion of the hair on the woman's head, it's pure.

23:10 Cloak that had contracted impurity of a Zav was afterwards made into a curtain, it is purified from that impurity.

24:10 Cloth pillow contracted Midras impurity, made into cloak or vice versa, impure due to Midras as it was before.

25:1 All flat wooden implements made to sit, lie, or ride upon are susceptible to Midras impurity: bed, chair, etc.

26:14 Even when an entire bed contracted impurity, if it was immersed component by component, it is pure

27:4 Bent shield: gets Midras impurity. Stadium sport shield: human corpse impurity. Arabs' play-shield: entirely pure.

28:5 Pouch w/ inner pouch, 1 of the 2 contracted impurity due to impure liquids, the other does not contract impurity.

#Mikvaot

1:10 For Mikva immersion, visible portions of body must be in contact with water. But must still clean folds of body.

2:6 Loose necklaces don't intervene, don't strangle. Tight ones intervene; women choke themselves w/ them to look fat.

3:24 When immerse laundered clothes, the water must penetrate through them to the extent that air bubbles arise.

4:7 Mikva had exactly 40 Se'ah, added Se'ah of drawn water, then removed Se'ah of water from it, Mikveh is acceptable.

5:6 Cistern full w/ drawn water, canal of rainwater flows thru. Pasul until determine if 3 Lugim of drawn water remain.

6:7 When either a sponge or a bucket that contains 3 Lugim of drawn water falls into a Mikveh, doesn't disqualify it.

7:12 If Mikva color changes on its own w/o anything falling in, ok. Disqualified if color changed due to other liquid.

8:11 Anything created from the water, e.g., red worms, ok for immersion. One may immerse in the eye of a giant fish.

9:18 Can't immerse in wave crest when it's in air before falls. If 2 ends of a wave are touching earth, ok to immerse.

10:3 Left empty Mikva, returned, found it full, it's acceptable. There's a doubt if the water for this Mikva was drawn.

11:12 Mikva immersion is Scriptural decree, needs proper intent of heart. Immersed w/o intent to purify, disqualified.

11. SEFER NEZIKIN

BOOK OF DAMAGES

#NizkeiMamon

1:1 Owner is responsible for all damage done by his animal.

2:2 Private property damaged by pebbles kicked by animal walking -- owner pays half.

3:1 Animal eats someone else's produce: in private property owner pays full damage.

4:1 If owner took normal precautions but the animal escaped and damaged, owner blameless.

5:1 Animal wanders in field, farmer warns owner 3 times, then slaughters animal and tells owner "here's the meat."

6:6 "Muad" (forewarned) animal that is sold or given as a gift reclaims status of a "Tam" (simple, placid) animal.

7:3 Animal that hurt a person, the owner pays damages, but not for pain, work stoppage, medical or embarrassment.

8:6 Ox did damage & owner sold it, plaintiff gets damages of value of ox from buyer & buyer reclaims from seller.

9:1 1st ox chasing 2nd. 2nd ox got hurt. Owner of 2nd says to 1st: your fault. 1st says: don't know. No payment.

10:11 Man enters private property without permission & killed by animal, owner doesn't have to make restitution.

11:9 An ox that killed a man and was sentenced to death, any sale, gift or transfer of ox ownership is invalid.

12:10 Man dug pit 10 handbreaths or more, liable for death of animal that falls in. Not liable for death if less.

13:2 Obstacles left in the public path have the same laws as a "pit". The person who left it pays for all damages.

14:2 Started fire in own field, spread to neighbor's field, liable, unless unlikely it would have spread (river).

#Geneiva

1:3 "Ganav" a thief who steals without owners knowing. "Gazlan" a robber who takes by force with victim's knowledge.

2:1 A Jew that steals from a non-Jew or from Temple property must repay the principal, but not the "double" fine.

3:1 Person whose act merits both capital punishment & financial penalty, only receives capital punishment.

4:1 Guard swore item wasn't by him, took it for himself & witnesses testified that it was by him, pays double.

5:1 Don't buy stolen goods. Severe sin. Encourages thieves to steal more. Proverbs 29:24: "hates his own soul."

6:2 If shepherd sells item that would be noticed by owner, can buy from him. If wouldn't be noticed, considered stolen.

7:1 Weights and measures must be exact. Anything less is deceiving others.

8:1 Just as with scales, weights & measures, also need to be exact with land. Even a fingerbreadth of land great loss.

9:12 Trespasser into garden, field, pen or corral (as opposed to a house) may not be killed by owner.

#Gezela

1:10 Just the desire to get home, wife, utensils or anything else of his fellow, even legally, violates "Don't covet."

2:1 Stolen object that has not changed, object itself must be returned. If changed, returns value of object.

3:1 Object thief stole rose in value & thief damaged it, pays increased value. Otherwise, pays value at time of theft.

4:1 Robber fined that victim swears about what was stolen & if there are witnesses to a theft robber pays entire claim.

5:18 A king whose currency is accepted throughout the land is a true king. If not, he's a thief & his laws aren't valid.

6:10 Rabbis prohibited gambling. It's like stealing, even if participants know & agree beforehand that can lose money.

7:1 Jew denies that he owes money to a Jew. Swore falsely. Has to pay back the principal plus 1/5th & bring a sacrifice.

8:5 Stole from a convert & swore falsely, if convert died without inheritors, pays Kohanim principal +1/5 + sacrifice.

9:1 Robbed property & damaged it, robber must return property to original condition or add to the difference in value.

10:1 If non-Jew seized field of Jew with cause & then sold it to another Jew, 1st Jew has no claim to land.

11:1 Positive command to return lost object to fellow Jew. If doesn't, violates prohibition & negates positive command.

12:1 A person's own lost object has priority over that of anyone else, if can't also return the other person's object.

13:1 Lost objects that are returnable: the finder needs to publicize it & ask for identifying signs to give it back.

14:2 Lost object with no identifying marks: when owner realizes lost, despairs of ever finding it. Finder can keep it.

15:1 Finds object that seem intentionally placed down, can't touch it, even if doesn't have identifying mark.

16:1 Needles, nails or the like: found 1, can keep; found 2 or more, needs to announce. Number of items like a mark.

17:1 Whenever talked about finding a lost article, only becomes finder's property when reaches his hand or his domain.

18:13 Found contract. If possible the obligation already fulfilled, don't return contract, lest try to make 2nd claim.

#Hovel

1:1 When injure someone liable for 5 things: damages, pain, medical treatment, loss of work and embarrassment suffered.

2:14 To determine medical expenses, estimate days condition will last & requirements to treat. Damager pays immediately.

3:7 Grave sin: "Whoever embarrasses someone publicly with words doesn't have a share in the world to come."

4:7 Hit own parent: if didn't draw blood, owe the 5 payments; if drew blood, doesn't owe because punishment is execution.

5:2 Can't raise hand in threatening way against another, even if don't hit them. Considered a wicked person if does so.

6:8 Guy with beam walking behind guy with jug. If beam breaks jug, owner of beam is liable.

7:7 One is fully liable for any damages that caused indirectly (i.e. removed pillow from under falling utensils).

8:14 Person pursuing a murderer in act of attacking 3rd party is not liable for any incidental damage, so won't hesitate.

#Rozeah

1:7 Better to stop a potential murderer "Rodef" non-fatally, but if not sure will stop them, commanded to kill them.

2:4 King or court allowed to kill assassin contractor even if technically they are not deserving of the death penalty.

3:3 Man died from blow of object: court checks object, strength of blow, attacker, victim & likelihood of death.

4:8 Murderer who can't be executed because of technicality: imprisoned, fed little, then fed barley until belly bursts.

5:1 Killed unintentionally, exiled to City of Refuge. Court can't accept ransom from killer to stay in his own city.

6:4 If someone was killed due to negligence, murderer is not accepted to City of Refuge & blood redeemer can kill him.

7:8 Admitted to City of Refuge, prohibited to leave, even for great need of nation. Only freed when Kohen Gadol dies.

8:10 Other 42 Levite cities serve as cities of refuge, but the 6 main Cities of Refuge are havens even without intent.

9:2 Murdered corpse discovered. Buried where found. Elders of nearest city bring calf (egla arufa) to riverbank.

10:9 Elders decapitate calf by riverbank. Can never farm that area. Can comb flax, drill stones (i.e. non-farming work).

11:4 Must build strong guardrail 10 Tefah high on roof & any potentially dangerous location on ones property.

12:4 Don't put coins in mouth. May have dried spittle of sick person or sweat. All sweat is like venom except from face.

13:1 Friend's animal falling under its load, command to help him unload the animal whether load is too much or not.

12. SEFER KINYAN

BOOK OF ACQUISITION

#Mehira

1:3 Land is acquired in one of 3 ways: money transfer, contract of sale, or Hazaka (demonstrating one's ownership).

2:7 Sells or gifts herd & gives over the Mashkuhit (animal that leads the herd), enough for other to acquire whole herd.

3:4 Paid for object, can retract if didn't lift it. Buyer lifted object that usually don't lift, acquires it & must pay.

4:1 A person's container acquires articles placed in it wherever he has permission to put the container.

5:1 Barter transaction binding once 1 side lifts object, even if traders assign different monetary values to each item.

6:1 Produce can't be used, but can be acquired in barter trade. Coins can't be given or acquired in barter transaction.

7:2 Transaction that agreed but not completed, whoever backs out gets curse of "Mi Shepara" (God will take retribution).

8:1 Agreement as to sale price of field; buyer paid part; buyer doesn't acquire the whole field until pays in full.

9:3 Orphan's property same rules as Temple property. If orphan sells produce & didn't receive money, can retract sale.

10:1 Person forced to sell item, binding. Seller protested prior in front of witnesses that against will, not binding.

11:2 A sale done based on some condition, only works if a regular transfer is done first & then the condition fulfilled.

12:11 Buyer can retract if seller took advantage, for as long as takes to show merchandise to expert for appraisal.

13:4 Seller transparent about the price of the item & the value of the item: even if large difference, not unfair gain.

14:18 Verbal abuse is more severe than unfair gain. Verbal abuse can't be compensated. God responds promptly if called.

15:5 If conducts business without making specific demands, assume he's following prevailing customs of the community.

16:9 Sold article with defect that couldn't see, if article destroyed due to defect, seller has to reimburse the buyer.

17:1 Said merchandise was good but turned out bad; buyer can retract. Bad, but turned out good; seller can retract.

18:1 It's forbidden to deceive in business, whether to a Jew or a non-Jew. Seller must notify buyer of all defects.

19:1 Can't sell property or object that is disputed or under judgement until buyer is made fully aware of the situation.

20:1 Disagree on price, then reunite: if buyer takes object, seller's price; but if seller gives it over, buyer's price.

21:1 Can sell (@ market price) even if don't know item's measure, weight or quantity. If don't even know WHAT it is, no.

22:1 Can't make sale, gift or will of item not yet in existence: produce of field, fruit of trees, offspring of animals.

23:1 Can transfer ownership of property with regard to the produce it will give. Like renting a house.

24:15 If seller didn't write "from ground of earth's depths to heights of the sky" buyer won't get air or depth rights.

25:2 Sold house: doesn't include other structures, large roof, cistern, even if on property, unless specifically stated.

26:4 Seller of land needs to buy from the buyer a path to get to his well, winepress or dovecote that kept in field.

27:1 If sold ship, doesn't include attached small boats, servants or any of the merchandise unless specifically says so.

28:5 "I'm selling you land of a specific size." Must be exact. If less, pay buyer. If more, return extra land to seller.

29:18 A drunk liable for actions. Selling, buying & gifts binding. If drunk like Lot, considered mentally incapacitated.

30:1 If someone acquires land or item for person w/o their knowledge, beneficiary can decline; seller can't retract.

#Zehia

1:1 Items found in desert or by river like grass, trees, wild fruit are ownerless. 1st to take ownerless object owns it.

2:1 Land of convert who died w/o heirs, or of non-Jew that sold to Jew that didn't claim, can be claimed by Hazaka.

3:2 If creditor forgoes debt or gives gift of object that beneficiary was guarding, verbal statement enough & binding.

4:8 One can acquire on behalf of minors or adults, w/ or w/o their presence. A person's courtyard acquires objects in it.

5:1 Gifting from someone healthy or sick, must always be done openly & publicly. Secret gift documents are of no value.

6:1 Gift given, assess & follow intent. Dad told that son died, signed over property to other, if son alive, gift null.

7:1 Shushvinut: $ sent by friends of groom (Shushvinim) for wedding expenses, who then eat & drink w/groom at party.

8:2 Shchiv mera: deathly ill bedridden person. His verbal orders are considered as if they were written & delivered.

9:1 Shchiv mera says don't reveal gift until after die, valid. It's not a secret gift, because after death will reveal.

10:7 Can't find $ father left. Had dream, told him place & instructions. Found $. Doesn't have to fulfill instructions.

11:24 If a Shchiv mera says don't eulogize me, not eulogized; if says don't use my money to bury me, ignored.

12:17 Righteous don't accept gifts. Rather they trust in God, not in generous people. "One who hates gifts will live."

#Shchenim

1:2 If can't divide property, 1 partner can say to other: Sell me your portion for this price, or buy mine for same.

2:12 Partners buy field & then divide it, neither has any rights in the side of the other. Can block water, windows.

3:9 Five gardens, 1 spring that gets damaged: all owners participate in repairs upstream to them, but not downstream.

4:1 House wall falls, loft owner has no responsibility; can compel house owner to rebuild wall to original strength.

5:1 Commonly-owned courtyard: partners can compel each other to build gatehouse, door; anything that is local custom.

6:1 Residents of city can compel each other to build wall; gates; bolt; synagogue; Torah, Prophets & Writings scrolls.

7:1 Built courtyard, can't ask neighbor to block up his window. Building wall, can't cast shadow on neighbor's window.

8:1 Building projection into neighbor's yard, neighbor can prevent. If doesn't prevent right away, it can stay there.

9:12 Owner of store below warehouse can't make it a bakery, paint factory, barn or anything that creates warm air.

10:2 Large threshing floor must be kept 50 cubits away from city, so wind won't carry winnowed straw & harm people.

11:1 Threshing floor, latrine, makes dust or dirt; must keep far enough that dirt, odor, dust doesn't bother neighbor.

12:3 Square plot to be divided, river E & N, road S & W, divide diagonally. If 1 wants 1 side, give if doesn't bother.

13:1 Land given as gift, rights of neighbor to buy that land don't apply; but only if truly a gift & not a deception.

14:5 Precedence in selling field to is the following order: Torah scholar / city neighbor / field neighbor / relative.

#Sheluhim

1:1 Appoints messenger to buy or sell property or items, messenger is empowered & all his transactions are binding.

2:2 Can appoint as agent a man; woman, even if married; servant or maidservant. Have intelligence & Mitzva obligation.

3:1 When have agent carry out legal proceedings, must compose power of attorney & perform act that grants agent power.

4:1 All means of acquiring that buyers use to buy, are used by partners to acquire assets contributed to partnership.

5:2 If partner violates agreement w/ merchandise: sells on credit, takes abroad, etc., takes loss, but splits profits.

6:1 If only one partner working, called Esek, investment agreement, as opposed to partnership, & has different laws.

7:2 If investment agreement initially loses money & then profits, only split money by calculating total.

8:1 Gave eggs to farmer for chickens to sit on eggs, hatch & raise chicks, must pay him wage even if splitting profit.

9:1 Even if no specific claim, partners, sharecroppers, legal guardians, family, all take oath: didn't take anything.

10:5 "Be careful with this law (of oaths partners take about losses), masters of instruction have erred with it."

#Avadim

1:1 "Hebrew servant" only thief w/o funds sold by court or impoverished man (doesn't have clothing) sold self willingly.

2:2 Servant sold by court serves 6 years from day sold. Works on Sabbatical year, but released on Jubilee year.

3:8 Hebrew servant that is a Kohen can't have ear pierced, as considered blemish that disqualifies from Temple service.

4:16 Whenever a person declares a condition against what is written in the Torah, his condition is nullified.

5:5 Tips of limbs that won't regenerate: 10 fingers & 10 toes, ears, nose, male organ, woman's breasts. Eyes & teeth.

6:1 Master wrote to 3rd party & gave bill of release of slave to 3rd party, slave is free, even if didn't get document.

7:1 Wording of bill of release of slave must be clear, that completely severs the connection between slave & his master.

8:9 If slave asks master to move to Israel, the master must move with him or sell the slave to someone going to Israel.

9:1 If a Jewish man has relations with a non-Jewish slave, child born of the union has the status of a non-Jewish slave.

13. Sefer Mishpatim

Book of Judgements

#Sechirut

1:1 Unpaid watchman takes oath blameless. Borrower makes restitution. Watchman/renter make restitution of lost/stolen.

2:1 3 laws of 4 watchmen applies to unconsecrated movable property of Jews. Excludes land, slaves & promissory notes.

3:1 Watchman says item broke/died & not his fault, if place where people present, brings witnesses & cleared of fault.

4:6 Rented ship, loaded 1/30th above cargo limit, sank, must pay owner for value of the ship. Same for cargo animals.

5:1 Rents donkey to ride or carry glass items; if dies, owner gives new donkey; if not, returns fee minus what rode.

6:3 Landlord must provide doors; fix windows, roof, beams; make bolt, lock & other basic needs that require craftsman.

7:1 Can make any stipulation when renting just like when sell. Renting is merely selling for a limited amount of time.

8:14 Planting field in crop-sharing deal: worker changed crop, must still pay what agreed even if poor production.

9:1 Can't force workers to come early & stay late if not local custom. Must follow local customs, like providing food.

10:3 Craftsman is paid watchman of customer's article, until says "finished job, take it," then unpaid watchman.

11:2 Withholding worker's wages like murder. Violates 5 commands: pay on time; don't oppress, steal, hold, delay wage.

12:14 Slave can't say his minor kids won't eat from produce of master's field that they're harvesting. Given by God.

13:7 Employee warned not to steal work of employer by neglecting his work slightly here & there, wasting work time.

#Fikadon

1:1 Borrowed utensils or animal, lost or stolen, even if beyond his control, must make restitution; unless normal use.

2:1 Borrowed article or animal, if it's stolen or lost but the lender is with him, borrower is not liable for damages.

3:1 Borrows cow, owner sends with son, agent or servant, & cow dies before arriving at borrower, borrower not liable.

4:3 Unpaid watchman put object in inappropriate place: stolen, lost or destroyed. Negligent & must make restitution.

5:3 Left article or fruit w/ watcher. Thieves stole in his presence. If he was quiet, didn't call out for help, liable.

6:1 Watchman's oath: took correct care, what happened, article not w/ him, didn't use article for self before event.

7:3 Watchman: don't deal w/ article (unless told to), even if value deteriorating, as owner may want to deal himself.

8:1 Watching animal or object; lost or stolen; says "I'll pay;" thief discovered; watcher gets payment from thief.

#**Malve**

1:1 Command to lend money to poor among Israel. Greater than charity. Torah warns severely against not lending to poor.

2:7 Can't lend money even to Torah scholar without witnesses unless received collateral. Better to have promissory note.

3:1 Can't take collateral from widow, whether rich or poor: if admits to debt, pays; denies debt, she must take an oath.

4:2 Just as forbidden to lend at interest to Jew, can't borrow, broker, guarantee, write or witness loans with interest.

5:1 Lending w/ interest only prohibited between Jews. Permitted to borrow or lend to or from a Gentile w/ interest.

6:1 If lends (to Jew) & payment has some addition, clause or benefit beyond principal, considered interest & prohibited.

7:9 Renter can ask owner for loan for improvement of field, store, ship, etc. & pays > amount; but not for operations.

8:1 Can't increase price of merchandise in exchange for delayed payment, i.e. pay now 100 zuz or pay later for 120 zuz.

9:1 Can't place order for produce before market price is set. Once set, can order, even if seller doesn't have on hand.

10:1 Can lend produce w/o conditions. Borrowed 10 Seah of wheat, must return 10 Seah of wheat, even if price increased.

11:1 If borrowed $ in front of witnesses, doesn't need to repay in front of witnesses. If says paid, must swear that did.

12:7 Can't appropriate land from minors, except if have authenticated deed of sale & after guardian appointed for minors.

13:2 Lender needs 3 proofs for court to get property of borrower: verify debt note; prove debtor away; owned by borrower.

14:2 Lender has promissory note, demands that borrower pay, borrower says paid already, court instructs borrower to pay.

15:6 If lender agreed that would accept borrower's word when says paid back loan, can't use promissory note to collect.

16:10 On promissory note written on front or back that paid in part or all, as if paid, even if in lender's possession.

17:3 Borrower died, lender died, lender's heirs can't collect debt from borrower's heirs. Can't swear that wasn't paid.

18:1 Lend w/o any stipulation, all debtor's land & movable property is on lien. Defaults, lender collects from property.

19:4 Damages expropriated from superior land, lenders collect from intermediate land, woman's Ketuba from inferior land.

20:1 Debtor has many debts, 1st lender expropriates property 1st, from borrower & creditors. Can take from later lenders.

21:1 Creditor expropriates field & increase in field value. If increase due to investment, creditor gets 1/2 of increase.

22:2 Borrower says promissory note forged: if he seems right, given time to prove; if not, pays. If finds proof, gets $.

23:4 Promissory note dated Shabat or Yom Kipur, assume postdated & valid. Known that legal documents not made on Shabat.

24:2 Scribe's fee paid by: borrower on loan, buyer on sale, woman on divorce, groom on marriage, sharecroppers & workers.

25:9 If 2 people take loan from same person on same promissory note, they're guarantors for each other. Same w/ partners.

26:5 Loan made w/ verbal pledge, borrower overseas, lender claims from guarantor, guarantor says: 1st prove didn't pay.

27:1 Jewish legal document: any language, can't be forged, can't add/subtract content, Jewish witnesses who can read it.

#**Toen**

1:1 Claim against person about movable property, person admits part of claim, pays that, swears doesn't owe rest & free.

2:2 Can't swear in court if: took false or unnecessary oaths, lends at interest, eats non-kosher meat, thief, gambler.

3:1 Prutah value: weight of half a barleycorn of pure silver. Two Me'in value: weight of 32 barleycorns of pure silver.

4:1 Gives biblical oath if accused of owing item with specific measure, weight or quantity & admits owing part of it.

5:12 Deaf-mute, mentally ill can't make claims & can't claim against them, can't take oaths or make restitution. Blind ok.

6:1 Court needs precise statements: litigant claims Maneh that lent, entrusted or stole, defendant must answer in kind.

7:1 Admitted in front of 2 about debt, not casually, but w/o appointing them as witnesses, still serves as testimony.

8:1 Presume that movable property belongs to person with physical possession, even if witnesses testify belonged to other.

9:1 Craftsman possesses item, don't presume it's his. Man claims w/ witnesses craftsman has his item, can reclaim w/ oath.

10:1 An animal that normally roams free, if a person grabs hold of it, the owner can reclaim it with witnesses and oath.

11:2 Believed owner of land, if have witnesses & used undisputed for > 3 years. Gives oath that rightfully his and keeps.

12:5 2 partners: 1 uses field years 1, 3, 5; other years 2, 4, 6; ownership not established. Have contract defining, ok.

13:1 Even if benefited from land 3 yrs, can't claim it: craftsmen, sharecropper, guardian, partner, spouse, son & father.

14:4 Thief's son claims owner sold to his dad, not admissible. Grandson can, if says he or his dad acquired, not grandpa.

15:3 Took field thinking was heir, discovered closer heir, needs to give field to closer heir & pay for all that consumed.

16:1 If signed as witness for deed of sale, can't afterwards protest ownership of field saying seller stole it from you.

#Nahalot

1:3 Inheritance order: sons, descendants of sons, daughters, her descendants, father, brothers, grandfather & so on.

2:1 Firstborn gets x2 portion of father's estate. Example: 5 sons, 1st born gets 1/3 of estate, 4 others get 1/6 each.

3:1 1stborn doesn't get 2x portion of property owed to father. Gets = share to brothers of funds collected after death.

4:2 If a father declares person known as his son isn't his son: doesn't get inheritance, but doesn't make him a Mamzer.

5:2 Big estate: girls get upkeep, tenth of estate for dowry; boys inherit rest. Small estate: girls get upkeep, boys 0.

6:13 Don't differentiate between children during lifetime, even in small matters, so don't envy like Joseph's brothers.

7:1 Heard that man died, even though enough to permit wife to remarry, heirs don't inherit. They need clear proof.

8:1 Man missing, land to relative as share-cropper; not to kid so won't ruin. Kid's land not to relative, so won't rob.

9:2 Brothers share inherited estate, brother uses own funds to increase value, he gets profit. Otherwise share equally.

10:1 2 bros divide estate & 3rd shows up, or 3 bros divide estate & creditor takes part. Recalculate division equally.

11:1 Court gives orphans' $ to trustworthy person, invest in very low risk deals. Judges decide orphans' best interest.

14. SEFER SHOFTIM

BOOK OF JUDGES

#Sanhedrin

1:1-2 Must appoint court judges & officers of law in every city & region in Israel, but not outside of Israel.

2:1 Appoint to Sanhedrin only men of wisdom, understanding, great Torah knowledge, intellect, worldly & of lineage.

3:2 Sanhedrin didn't need to always be together. Could work & only join for gatherings. But always minimum of 23.

4:15 Unfit to judge 'cuz doesn't know or poor character, even if appointed by Exilarch or court, has no authority.

5:9 Diaspora court only handle common cases that involve financial loss: liability, loans, property damage. No fines.

6:9 Plaintiff can force other party to travel to court of great sage to hear their case. Was ongoing custom in Spain.

7:1 Litigant chooses judge, 2nd litigant chooses 2nd judge. 2 judges choose 3rd judge & together all 3 rule the case.

8:1 $ cases: simple majority decides verdict. Capital cases: simple majority for innocence, >2 difference for guilt.

9:1 ALL Sanhedrin judges find person liable in capital case, acquitted. Only executed if minority finds innocence.

10:1 In capital case, judge must follow his own opinion & not be swayed by opinion of others. Biblical transgression.

11:5 Mesit, person who entices to idolatry, own rules: entrap, not warned, no mercy. Cruelty to them mercy for world.

12:2 Sinner warned to see if inadvertent or intentional sin. Sinner says understands that liable w/ death, executed.

13:2 On way to execution, confesses, given frankincense in wine. Loses control of mind, becomes drunk, then killed.

14:1 4 death penalties: stone, burn, decapitate & strangle. Non-explicit penalty is strangling. Murderer decapitated.

15:1 Stoning: Disrobe man, hands tied, push off 2nd floor. Not dead, drop big stone on heart. Not dead, small stones.

16:1 Just as Mitzva to execute whoever obligated to execute, so, too, Mitzva to lash whoever obligated to get lashed.

17:5 If in middle of (not before) getting lashed subject defecates or urinates, not given further lashes. Degraded.

18:6 Don't execute or lash based on confession. Only w/ 2 witnesses. May be suicidal & just wants court to kill him.

19:1-4 21 prohibitions get Karet, court lashes. 18 prohibitions get Death by Heaven, get lashes. 168 just lashes.

20:1 Man pursued other, then see pursued in death throes & sword in killer's hand, but didn't see act, not testimony.

21:6 Priority of seeing cases: orphan, widow, Torah scholar, commoner. Woman before man; her shame is greater.

22:7 After leaving court, judge forbidden to say: I found you innocent, or liable, but my colleagues outnumbered me.

23:1-2 Can't get or give bribe. Even if was going to rule in favor of briber anyway. "Cursed is he who takes bribe."

24:2 Number of courts weren't fair increased, or were fair but not competent, agreed not to judge w/o firm knowledge.

25:9 Don't issue court summon months of Nisan & Tishrei 'cuz holiday preparations; or Fridays or day before holiday.

26:7 Jew doesn't recognize validity of Jewish court, get permission from Jewish court & can sue him in gentile court.

#**Edut**

1:1 Obligation for witness to testify whether makes liable or vindicates. Monetary cases only have to testify if summoned.

2:1 Hakirot/Drishot: more important questioning. Bedikot: nuanced questions. Hakirot/Drishot must know answers & match.

3:1 Sages: For witnesses in simple financial cases, don't ask intense Hakira/Drisha questions, so as not to prevent loans.

4:1 Capital case: 2 witnesses must see act & each other at same time & testify in court at same time. Otherwise invalid.

5:1 Ruling never made based on the testimony of only one witness, not for financial cases and not for capital punishment.

6:5 Court never checks if other court validated document correctly. Must assume they're knowledgeable & made no mistakes.

7:2 Accept testimony of men for what saw as minors: signatures of father, brother, teacher. Need other that knew as adult.

8:1 Asked to testify as to signature on promissory note, recognizes signature, but no recollection of case, can't testify.

9:1 Can't testify: women, slaves, minors, fools, deaf/mutes, blind, wicked, debased, relatives or has vested interest.

10:4 Wicked that can't testify: thieves, lying witnesses, borrow or lend w/ interest, shepherds, tax-collectors, gamblers.

11:3 Torah scholar acceptable as a witness unless disqualified. Boor unacceptable witness unless established as ethical.

12:2 Can't disqualify self as witness by incriminating self. Don't believe him about self, do believe about someone else.

13:1 Relatives can't testify together or for each other: fathers w/ son, grandson; brothers; cousins; uncles w/ nephews.

14:1 Witness disqualified from testimony because of marriage to relative; if wife died, even if had sons, can now testify.

15:1 If may have any benefit from testifying about case, can't testify or judge case; even city resident on city matters.

16:4 Judge needs to understand & determine if witness gets any benefit from testimony, even if unusual or far-fetched.

17:1 Even if wise, righteous men said witnessed person sin or borrow money, 1 can't testify to what didn't personally see.

18:1 Ed Zomem, false witness: testifies, others testify impossible for them to have witnessed. Get punishment of victim.

19:1 Ed Zomem found guilty even if highly unlikely (but not completely impossible) that could have witnessed what claimed.

20:2 Ed Zomem only executed if caught after innocent sentenced but before executed. If innocent executed, they're not.

21:2 Ed Zomem accuse person of owing debt sooner than reality & caught, they pay value of debt for period would have lost.

22:5 Plaintiff brings false witnesses, even 100 pairs, & true witnesses, if accurate, believe testimony of true witnesses.

#Mamrim

1:1 Sanhedrin essence of Oral Torah. Laws go out to all nation. If believe in Moshe & his Torah, must rely on Sanhedrin.

2:2 Sanhedrin issued edict, decree or custom & it spread throughout Israel, only a greater Sanhedrin can nullify it.

3:5 Rebel Elder: kill if sage differs w/ Sanhedrin on Mitzva that liable Karet & instructs others or does himself.

4:2 Rebel Elder liable if dispute can lead to violation of Karet. i.e. confusion on date, status of wife, $, sacrifice.

5:15 Not only can't hit or curse parents, also can't shame, even with words or even insinuation. Will be cursed by God.

6:10 Parents mentally ill, child treats them at their level. If so bad & can't handle, get others to take care of them.

7:2 Rebel Son: steals $ from dad, buys cheap meat & wine, eats outside home w/ group of fools, meat 1/2 raw, thin wine.

#Avel

1:1 Biblically must mourn 1st day of death & burial. Moshe instituted 7 days of mourning (& 7 days wedding celebrations).

2:1 Biblically mourn for mom, dad, son, daughter, paternal brother & sister. Rabbis added spouse, maternal bro & sis.

3:1 Except for the 6 relatives, if Kohen comes in contact with a corpse on purpose, after warned & witnesses, he's lashed.

4:4 Tombstone placed on grave. Righteous don't need tombstone, their words will be their memory & shouldn't visit graves.

5:20 Mourners: Can't greet, have lengthy or frivolous talks. Don't hold baby, causes laughter. Don't go to celebrations.

6:2 Mourner prohibited during 1st 30 days to: cut hair; wear freshly ironed clothes; marry; go to party; business travel.

7:1 Notified that relative died after <30 days = day of burial, keeps regular mourning. After >30 days, 1 day of mourning.

8:4 Don't inform the seriously ill if close relative died. Silence women who can't control themselves in their presence.

9:2 Tear clothing for ones Rabbi; Nasi; Av Bet Din; a community; blasphemy; burned Torah; over Judah, Jerusalem & Temple.

10:1 Shabat day of mourning, but no public mourning, only private: veiling head, marital relations, washing w/ hot water.

11:7 7 days of wedding celebration like Festival. If relative dies in middle, complete 7 days of celebration, then mourn.

12:2 Sluggish for sages' eulogy, won't live long; for upright person's, deserves death; if shed tears, God guards reward.

13:11 Don't mourn excessively. Death is pattern of the world. Proper to weep 3 days, eulogize 7, keep restrictions 30.

14:2 Accompanying guests is greater than hospitality which is greater than receiving God. Didn't accompany = shed blood.

#Melahim

1:8 If prophet appoints king from non-Judah tribe, if follows Torah & fights God's wars, considered king & rules apply.

2:1 Must honor & be in awe of king. Don't ride horse, sit on throne, use scepter, wear crown. Burn his things when die.

3:1 King write Torah for self besides 1 everyone should have. Always w/ him except in bathroom, etc. Read all his life.

4:1 King can raise taxes for his needs or for war. Can tax merchandise. Can confiscate property of or kill tax evaders.

5:9 Only leave Israel to study Torah, marry or save property; did it, must return. Can go on biz trips or if famine.

6:7 When place siege around city to conquer it, don't surround on all 4 sides; just on 3. Leave place for them to flee.

7:4 After fearful told to leave war & left, officers can chop leg of any further deserters. Flight beginning of defeat.

8:1 Jewish soldiers conquer non-Jewish area, can eat non-kosher meat & animals, if hungry & nothing else available.

9:14 Non-Jews fulfill command to set up courts: Put judges in major cities, judge & admonish on other 6 Noahide laws.

10:3 Gentile converted to Judaism, circumcised & immersed in Mikveh; if after decides that wants to forsake, can't.

11:4 Davidic king, observes Torah, gets Israel to follow, fights God's wars, builds Temple, gathers exile, he's Masiah.

12:2 Don't try to calculate Masiah's arrival. Sages cursed those who try to figure out arrival that they should die.

end

**End Maimonides'
Mishne Torah.
We shall return to you.**

#AboutTheAuthor

#Ben-Tzion Spitz, prolific writer on biblical & rabbinic themes.

#Former Chief Rabbi of Uruguay

#blog at torah.works and tweetyomi.org

#twitter @bentzis

#publisher: valiantpublishing.com

www.ingramcontent.com/pod-product-compliance
Lightning Source LLC
Chambersburg PA
CBHW051823040426
42447CB00006B/346